FROM SANTA FE TO

O'Keeffe Country

FROM SANTA FE TO *O'Keeffe Country*

A One Day Journey
Through the Soul of New Mexico

Rhoda Barkan and Peter Sinclaire

Illustrations by John D. Rice Jr.

Adventure Roads Travel / OCEAN TREE BOOKS

Adventure Ro

SANTA FE C

DISCOVERII

TWO HOURS BEYOND ATLANTA (Lincoln S. Bates)

FROM SANTA FE TO O'KEEFFE COUNTRY (Barkan, Sinclaire)

Published by:

OCEAN TREE BOOKS
Post Office Box 1295
Santa Fe, New Mexico 87504
(505) 983-1412

Cover Art by John D. Rice, Jr.
Design by Richard Polese and Sara Benjamin-Rhodes

---

*To reach Peter Sinclaire about his guide services in New Mexico,
call Santa Fe Tours, (505) 988-2774.*

ISBN 0-943734-32-0

Library of Congress Cataloging in Publication data:

Barkan, Rhoda, 1928-1997
    From Santa Fe to O'Keeffe Country: a one day journey through the
soul of New Mexico / Rhoda Barkan and Peter Sinclaire; illustrations by
John D. Rice Jr.
        p.   cm. — (Adventure Roads Travel)
    Includes bibliographical references.
    ISBN 0-943734-32-0
    1. Santa Fe Region (N.M.)—Tours. 2. O'Keeffe, Georgia, 1887-1986 —
Homes and haunts — New Mexico — Santa Fe Region — Guidebooks.
I. Sinclaire, Peter, 1950-   . II. Title. III. Series.
F804.S23.B37   1996
917.89'560453—dc20   96-28651
                                                          CIP

For Jason, Matthew, Kerry, Ashley, Benjamin, and Stacy.

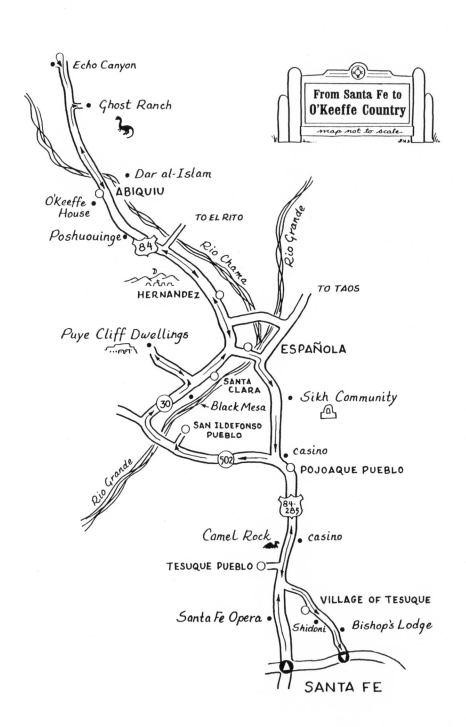

Echo Canyon

Ghost Ranch

Dar al-Islam

O'Keeffe House

ABIQUIU

Poshuouinge

TO EL RITO

Rio Chama

84

HERNANDEZ

Rio Grande

TO TAOS

Puye Cliff Dwellings

ESPAÑOLA

SANTA CLARA

Black Mesa

30

Sikh Community

SAN ILDEFONSO PUEBLO

Rio Grande

502

casino

POJOAQUE PUEBLO

84-285

Camel Rock

casino

TESUQUE PUEBLO

VILLAGE OF TESUQUE

Santa Fe Opera

Shidoni

Bishop's Lodge

SANTA FE

From Santa Fe to O'Keeffe Country

map not to scale

CONTENTS

PREFACE

ON A RAINY DAY in November of 1994, two Santa Fe friends set out for a drive. We were off to enjoy a few of the many sights in a part of northern New Mexico where Peter, as part of his job as a certified tour guide, had been hundreds of times before. Yet there was something special about this outing.

As we drove along, the exciting and intriguing things about people and places, diverse cultures, dramatic history and the area's exquisite beauty, inspired us to think about sharing our delight with others in a book. While passing in the shadows of mesas and gazing across colorful canyons, we realized that this one route captured much of what is quintessential about New Mexico. Although it would take a lifetime to really explore and know the state, if one had but a single day, *this* would be an ideal trip.

The journey of discovery you'll make is not unlike the one made by one of America's most well-known artists, Georgia O'Keeffe. As she motored north from Santa Fe, she became so enchanted by the landscape that she then painted it for the rest of her long life.

Rhoda's art history, newspaper background and her experience as a docent at Santa Fe's history and art museums complemented Peter's experience and knowledge of northern New Mexico. We joined forces and then enlisted the help of Richard Polese, publisher at Ocean Tree Books and president of the New Mexico Book Association. John D. Rice Jr., a talented Santa Fe landscape artist, offered to illustrate what we were putting into words.

As the book neared publication, an agreement was reached between the Museum of New Mexico, the Georgia O'Keeffe Foundation, and the Burnett-Tandy Foundation to open a museum in Santa Fe dedicated to O'Keeffe's life and work. The **Georgia O'Keeffe Museum** is at 217 Johnson Street in Santa Fe, just a few blocks from where this guidebook's route begins. Call 995-0785 for current hours. Admission at this writing is five dollars.

While *From Santa Fe to O'Keeffe Country* deals with only one small part of a very large state, we feel it will give you a sense not only of

New Mexico's larger landscape, but of the people, cultures, and history which are as much as part of the story as the spectacular and enchanting vistas. This guide is written with the armchair traveler in mind as well as for those who take the journey. For both, we hope our book will prove to be an indispensable travel companion.

—Rhoda Barkan and Peter Sinclaire

Acknowledgements

The authors wish to thank Charles Bennett, Linda Clarke, David Connolly, Adrian Garcia, Andrea Mildenberger, John D. Rice Jr., Orlando Romero, Eleanor Sinclaire, Peggy van Hulsteyn, Betsy Walker, and Michelle Wyler; and the staffs at the Library of the Laboratory of Anthropology, New Mexico State Library, and the Santa Fe Public Library, for their technical and professional assistance. Special thanks to Alfred, Amy and Susanne for their excellent advice and continuing support.

ABOUT THIS GUIDE

THIS ONE-DAY, self-guided tour is an invitation to experience the beauty and variety of the northern New Mexico landscape, and on the way acquire a deeper and more intimate understanding and appreciation of its peoples' history and culture. The guidebook you hold in your hands will help you accomplish this through a well-planned exploration of a part of the state which we believe reveals an essence of the whole.

Your journey begins at the corner of Paseo de Peralta and Guadalupe Street, just a few blocks northwest of Santa Fe's historic Plaza, and 7/10 mile from where US 84/285 heads north. The out-going route, if you visit all suggested places, covers approximately 95 miles (158 kilometers) one way; the return route is only 67 miles (111 kilometers). Your tour climaxes in a strikingly beautiful area often referred to as "O'Keeffe Country." Easy-to-read maps, with mileage between places and areas of interest, are provided for each part. Please note that these maps are not to scale.

Significant things to see and do are called "Sites" and "Stops." *Sites* are places and things that can be enjoyed from the car; *Stops* are places and things best enjoyed by getting out of the car for up-close exploration. The trip has been designed as a seven-hour excursion; however, depending on your interests and the actual itinerary you choose, it may take a little longer.

Every season presents delights. Inclement weather won't hamper a satisfying view of suggested Sites and Stops from the comfort of your car. A four-wheel-drive vehicle may facilitate traversing one or two dirts roads off the main highways, but it's not essential. Special interests are kept in mind, allowing you to customize your trip.

Birders, hikers, natural history and archaeology buffs, and those with an adventurous bent are advised to wear appropriate footwear, carry water, and dress in layers. Rain or snow showers can occur unexpectedly in any season, and rapid temperature changes may result. As the sun goes down, so does the temperature— sometimes as much as 15 to 20 degrees even during summer months.

If you wish to visit Puye Cliff Dwellings (and we hope you will), plan to spend about one hour at this ancient ruin. Therefore, your tour will probably run longer than seven hours, unless only brief visits to the other Stops are made.

You'll find symbols accompanying the text, indicating birding sites, flora and fauna, gas stations, geological formations, hiking trails, special photo opportunities, picnic spots, restaurants, and restrooms.

A glossary and pronunciation guide, calendar of Pueblo events and a guide to Pueblo etiquette, a list of favorite restaurants, birding tips, hiking trails, stories to entertain young travelers, and our recommended reading list are found at the back of the book.

Admission fees are not required at most of the Stops described in this book. The few exceptions are noted in the text.

¡Vaya con Dios!

Key to Symbols:

 Birding Site

 Photo Opportunity

 Flora and Fauna

 Picnic Spot

 Gasoline

 Restaurants

 Geological Formations

 Restrooms

 Hiking Trail

AN EVER-PRESENT PAST

JUST BEYOND the southwestern city limits of Santa Fe, a prehistoric camel left its footprints in soft volcanic mud, deposited in the wake of the violent creation of the Jemez Mountains to the north and west. Millennia before this creature took its stroll, colliding continental plates squeezed the towering Sangre de Cristo Mountains skyward to the east.

Not far from the camel tracks, archaeologists recently unearthed evidence of an Archaic band of native people. This discovery pushed back known habitation of the Santa Fe area well before the pit-house dwellers and their successors, the Anasazi, who occupied this area a thousand or more years ago.

The vast open, quiet spaces of New Mexico belie a dynamic evolutionary history. Mysteries of antiquity—human, natural, and geological—abound here, awaiting discovery in the distant mesas, mountains and arroyos.

On your one-day trip from Santa Fe to O'Keeffe Country you will meet a people who claim their Anasazi ancestors inhabited the starkly beautiful plateaus and mesas of the Rio Grande Valley between A.D. 1200 and 1400. We do not know what name these ancient Pueblo (town) people called themselves, but the Navajo word *Anasazi* (the ancient ones) has been acknowledged by today's Pueblo people and accepted by most historians and archaeologists.

Milder winters and increased rainfall possibly allowed former hunter-gatherers to evolve into an agrarian society. Archaeological studies indicate the Anasazi cultivated corn, beans and squash, hunted small animals, made pottery, fashioned simple tools, wove cotton garments, and created images on rocks that reflected their connection to a spiritual world.

The nomadic Apache and Navajo people came into New Mexico from the north sometime after A.D. 1100. Primarily hunters, they moved their temporary dwellings in seasonal migrations. When herds of large animals diminished, some of these Indians became warring bands in order to survive. They attacked established Pueblo

13

communities where crops were often abundant. These conflicts became more complicated with the arrival of a new people.

Spanish exploration of the North American continent was sparked by the successful conquest of a rich Aztec culture in Mexico in 1520. Expeditions came north looking for Cibola—the purported seven cities of gold, which the Spanish had not found among Aztec or Incan civilizations.

Exploration, conquest and colonization continued through the 16th century. Ever-present were Franciscan fathers. Their mission: to convert indigenous peoples to Catholicism and to maintain church traditions and practices among the Spanish settlers.

Although the region was explored as early as 1540, the first settlement in New Mexico was established just before 1600. Much-needed materials and supplies came up the 1500-mile Camino Real (Royal Road) from Mexico about once every three years. Plagued by drought, severe winters, measles, whooping cough, and smallpox (which was particularly virulent among the young), as well as attacks by nomadic Indian bands, these isolated Spanish communities barely survived.

After the Villa Real de Santa Fe (Royal Town of Holy Faith) was established as the capital in 1610 (newly discovered documents hint that a Spanish settlement existed there even earlier), power struggles developed between secular and ecclesiastic authorities. Religious persecution, taxation and forced labor imposed on Indian populations led to a major uprising in 1680. The Pueblo Revolt, which united the far-flung Pueblo communities of the Southwest, forced the Spanish to abandon the province.

Tewas and Tanos, Indian people speaking two different languages, occupied the *Casas Reales* (royal houses) in and around the Palace of the Governors in Santa Fe. And there they built traditional multi-storied dwellings and underground ceremonial chambers called kivas. The natives remained in the city until 1693, when Don Diego de Vargas, New Mexico's governor in exile, returned to permanently retake the Villa Real de Santa Fe in the name of the Spanish king.

A more reasonable approach to colonial governing came with the return of the Europeans. Systems of taxation, forced labor and religious persecution were relaxed or abolished. Within five years, physical conflicts between Spanish and Pueblo people ceased. Catholicism practiced at the pueblos came to include native spiritual rites, as it does to this day.

The 1700s ushered in a period of relative peace and accomodation; however threats to personal safety continued from old raiding enemies and new ones, the Comanches and Utes.

Yet another people were to come. In 1821 Mexico won its independence from Spain, and New Mexico became a northern province of Mexico. Under Spanish rule New Mexico's borders were closed to foreigners; under Mexican rule the Santa Fe Trail was opened to trade with an entrepreneurial United States. Finished goods, such as bricks, milled lumber, metal tools and implements, calico and lace, arrived from Missouri each year. Local traders exchanged gold, silver, beaver pelts, wool, and Indian blankets for American products.

Down this overland trading route, the Anglo-Americans drove their wagons, crossing the vast plains. These early westward journeys were filled with dangers: attacks by the Comanches, Apaches and Kiowas, brutal storms, and limited water. Yet, believing in America's Manifest Destiny, young men kept westering.

After 25 years of Mexican rule, New Mexico became part of the United States during the Mexican-American War. This conflict arose in 1846, ostensibly over the legal border between Texas and Mexico. Most historians now regard this war as a land grab by the Americans—part of an attempt to create a country that stretched "from sea to shining sea."

As a result of this war, New Mexico (which then included most of present-day Arizona) and California were included within the borders of the United States. New Mexico applied to become a state in 1850; Congress declined and chose to make this Spanish-speaking, Catholic land a U.S. Territory instead. For 62 years, the President and Congress of the United States, rather than the inhabitants of the territory, controlled New Mexico's destiny.

The colorful Territorial period (1846-1912) of New Mexico's history included cowboys and cattle, outlaws such as the notorious Henry McCarty (some called him Billy the Kid), and the arrival of the Atchison, Topeka and Santa Fe Railroad in 1880. Beginning with the assassination of John Slough, the Chief Justice of New Mexico Territory, outside the billiard room of the Exchange Hotel in Santa Fe in 1867, violence became very much part of the fabric of life and politics in New Mexico at least through the 1890s. From this period writers have found a wealth of events and personalities from which to fashion the legends of the frontier West.

In 1912 New Mexico at last achieved statehood, the 47th in number and fifth largest in area. The 20th century brought an influx of writers, poets, painters, photographers, and sculptors. Drawn to northern New Mexico by its moderate climate, the beauty of the landscape and the mixture of exotic cultures, these included such notables as D.H. Lawrence, Georgia O'Keeffe, Ansel Adams, Alan Houser, and Willa Cather. Their endeavors, as well as the works of many others, have attempted to reflect and express the colors, geologic wonders, cultural distinctiveness and spiritual essence of this special place. The timeless enchantment of New Mexico's north country continues to attract talented dreamers and incurable romantics from far and wide.

FROM SANTA FE TO

O'Keeffe Country

Part One ———————————————————————

SANTA FE TO THE RIO GRANDE

North through a Cultural Tapestry

Por la vereda, no hay quien se pierda.
(If you follow the path, you will not get lost.)

❁ **Approximate Time: 1½ hours**
Approximate Distance: 28 miles

YOU ARE ABOUT to take a journey into a distant past. On it you will see vestiges of ancient cultures and their modern-day descendants, a landscape that silently records a turbulent geologic history, villages with 300-year-old stories to tell, a place where unexpected religions have taken root and, of course, the setting in which one of America's most highly-acclaimed artists made her home.

Depart on your day's adventure from the corner of Paseo de Peralta (named for the first Spanish governor in Santa Fe) and Guadalupe Street, just a few blocks from the Plaza at the heart of Santa Fe. Century Bank is on the northwest corner of this intersection, with the DeVargas Center behind it. Albertsons, a large supermarket in this mall, is a convenient spot to pick up snacks and fixings for a picnic on your one-day trip.

Heading north on Guadalupe, you'll see **Rosario Cemetery** and its historic chapel on your right. Each year in June the little statue of *La Conquistadora* (Our Lady of Conquest) is carried in a religious procession from her home in St. Francis Cathedral to this sanctuary. Here she stays for a novena—special prayers said over a nine-day period. La Conquistadora is the oldest image of the Virgin Mary in the United States—a "saddle virgin" brought by missionaries on mules to the Spanish province of *Nuevo México* in 1626.

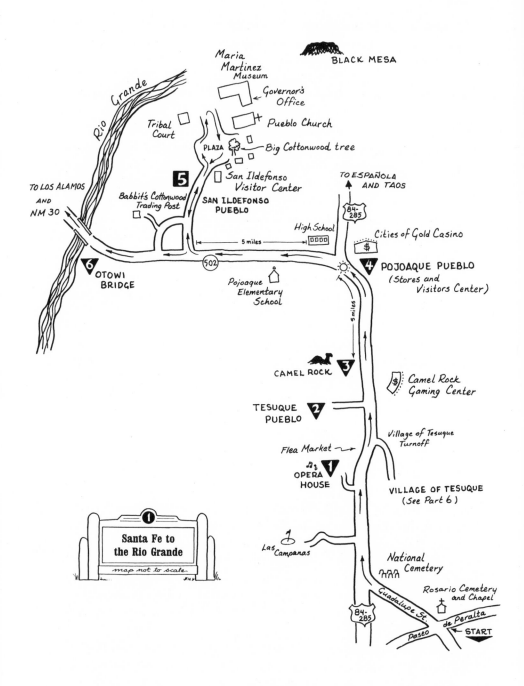

BLACK MESA

Rio Grande

Maria Martinez Museum

Governor's Office

Tribal Court

Pueblo Church

PLAZA

Big Cottonwood tree

San Ildefonso Visitor Center

TO ESPAÑOLA AND TAOS

5

Babbit's Cottonwood Trading Post

SAN ILDEFONSO PUEBLO

TO LOS ALAMOS AND NM 30

84-285

Cities of Gold Casino

$

High School

5 miles

502

6 OTOWI BRIDGE

Pojoaque Elementary School

4 POJOAQUE PUEBLO (Stores and Visitors Center)

5 miles

CAMEL ROCK

3

$ Camel Rock Gaming Center

TESUQUE PUEBLO

2

Village of Tesuque Turnoff

Flea Market →

♫ OPERA HOUSE

1

VILLAGE OF TESUQUE (See Part 6)

Las Campanas

National Cemetery

Rosario Cemetery and Chapel

Guadalupe St.

84-285

de Peralta

Paseo

▶ START

Santa Fe to the Rio Grande

map not to scale

Just beyond, orderly rows of tombstones in **Santa Fe National Cemetery** soon appear on the hillside. In this hallowed ground is the grave of Charles Bent, the first U.S. governor of New Mexico, appointed in 1846 by General Stephen Watts Kearny shortly after the Army of the West took the province from the Republic of Mexico. Bent was assassinated and scalped one year later by Taos residents who resisted American authority.

Remains of thirty young Confederate volunteers killed in the Battle of Glorieta Pass (21 miles southeast from Santa Fe) in 1862 also rest here. During a public ceremony in 1993, when their bodies were transferred from a primitive battlefield burial site, descendants and Civil War reenactors sprinkled Texas soil over their gravesites in the National Cemetery.

The route keeps climbing as it joins US Highways 84/285 just 7/10 mile from your starting point. Houses nestled in the hills on the northside of Santa Fe are usually valued well above the average price of a home in the city which today is close to $200,000. The *Las Campanas* sign you pass indicates a left-hand turn to an upscale golfing development with large estates six miles to the west. Its promoters say it's so quiet there you can hear the bells (*las campanas*) of St. Francis Cathedral ring in Santa Fe. Las Campanas boasts a golf layout credited to Jack Nicklaus, with plans for a second. Golf courses in this arid land are a source of bewilderment to most Santa Feans.

As you climb the grade, known locally as Tesuque Hill, look to the right where you'll notice large homes on hills in the distance; then ridges higher up with no homes at all. Where the houses end the Santa Fe National Forest and Tesuque Pueblo lands begin.

The **Sangre de Cristo Mountains** on the eastern horizon are the southernmost section of the Rocky Mountain chain. The Sangres stretch from southern Colorado to just south of Santa Fe. They were given their name, Blood of Christ, by the Spanish. When covered with snow they sometimes take on a reddish hue from the afterglow of sunset. In New Mexico you'll get as much pleasure looking to the east at sunset as to the west—even without snow!

These mountains were formed over 60 million years ago when the North American land mass collided with a Pacific Ocean plate and the land buckled in places. This region is one of those places. How high do you think the peaks are? Santa Fe's elevation is 7,000 feet above sea level. Here the Sangres rise to 12,000 feet, or about one mile above you.

Santa Feans and visitors "take to the hills" in winter when the mountains become a skiers' delight. Just 16 miles from the city one can enjoy the sport at the **Santa Fe Ski Basin** from Thanksgiving weekend until early to mid-April, as long as Mother Nature cooperates with sufficient snow (see *Part Six*).

As you drive north along US 84/285, piñon pine and juniper trees dot the terrain. Some may call them shrubs, but please don't make fun of New Mexico's trees! The piñon, the State Tree, is famous for its tasty nuts. These diminutive, slow-growing evergreens with short needles can live for many years before they produce a crop. In addition, it's often three to seven years between crops, depending on soil and weather conditions. Piñon nuts have become a delicacy, and sometimes a luxury due to their intermittent production. Piñon nut chocolate is a great gift to take home from the Southwest, but calorie counters beware: these nuts have more calories than chocolate.

Mixed in with the piñon trees are junipers: evergreens with spiny needles. Ancient peoples used the juniper berry as a "famine food" and cold remedy. Today their descendants prepare a tea from the berry to stop runny noses, stomach disorders, constipation and rheumatism. Some Pueblo women drink juniper tea during childbirth or immediately after delivery. Pharmacists also used a juniper compound to relieve cold symptoms. Others make gin with it. Thus, this rich woodland of pine and juniper has been a source of food, fuel and medicine for centuries.

Site 1: Santa Fe Opera 🎵 *"A Miracle of Sound"*

Music, drama, costumes, and stage design combine to make nighttime magic in an open-air theater set in the foothills of the mountains of northern New Mexico.

A sign indicating the turnoff for the Opera will come into view on your left. Seven miles from the city, a former guest ranch is now the home of the **Santa Fe Opera**. John Crosby, its founder and musical director, has rightfully claimed this "acoustically perfect amphitheater provides a miracle of sound."

Before construction of the opera house began, sound engineers fired rifles into the air to determine the location for the best acoustics. An unusual, open-air theater with bench seating for 480 was built. A reflecting pool separated the audience from the orchestra pit. Puccini's *Madama Butterfly* was the Santa Fe Opera's first offering on July 3, 1957. The twinkling lights from a not-too-distant Los Alamos appeared to mimic the lights of the opera's Nagasaki Harbor setting.

In July 1967 a disastrous fire destroyed the original opera house. Through the heroic efforts of the performers and the people of Santa Fe, the beleaguered company missed just a single performance as it continued its season in the local high school gymnasium. Igor Stravinsky served as honorary chairman of a National Emergency Committee organized to rebuild the facility. Some $2.4 million was quickly raised to create the present-day opera house which opened on time for its 1968 season.

The opera company draws voices and musicians from around the world. Its highly-regarded Apprentice Program provides a unique opportunity for young American singers to make their debuts. Some 500 seasonal employees are hired to craft both the beautiful stage settings and lavish costuming for which the Opera is known.

An original artistic profile has been developed by the Santa Fe Opera. American premieres and lesser known operas, as well as familiar favorites, are always included in the annual fare. The beauty of the setting, musical excellence, elegant costumes and dramatic staging have drawn an ever-increasing number of national and international opera-lovers. Annual audiences have grown from 12,000 to over 77,000. A budget of under $10,000 for its first season has grown to almost $5 million for the 41st season.

The Santa Fe Opera will get a dramatic full roof and other renovations by 1998. Its new covering will shelter even the formerly drench-prone expensive seats from the frequent thunderstorms of July and August. Seating will be increased to over 2,000. Ticket prices range from about $20 to just over $100. Backstage tours are available during opera season. Call the box office at (505) 986-5959 for performance and tour schedules and tickets. Opera goers are advised to bring warm clothing as curtains rise at 8:30 or 9 p.m. and Santa Fe is known for its cool, even chilly summer evenings.

Just after you've driven by the Opera House on the hillside to the left, you will see either an empty dirt lot or hundreds of parked vehicles, depending on the day of the week and the weather. This is **Trader Jack's Flea Market**, popular with locals and tourists alike. Flea market vendors sell items from all over the world. You may find Indian jewelry, African dashikis, old tools, Guatemalan serapes, local produce, or a rug dealer from Canyon Road. "The Flea" is free to the public. It's open on Friday, Saturday and Sunday from April to October, plus Saturday and Sunday during February, March and November. Go early Saturday morning for good parking. Trader Jack says his flea is "the most beautiful market in the world." Its setting in the foothills of the Sangre de Cristos is indeed spectacular.

Site 2: Tesuque Pueblo ୬ *A Sovereign Land*

As you descend the hill, you may feel you've left familiar territory—and you have! In a sense, you've left New Mexico. This is *Pueblo Indian* land, where the laws are different. On either side of the highway you are subject to tribal and federal laws. The highway here is patrolled by both state and tribal police. These lands belong to **Tesuque Pueblo**, one of nineteen pueblos within the state's borders. Each is a separate sovereign entity. All are related by cultural characteristics and traditions, but have their own laws, customs and ceremonial days. Some pueblos share one of the five puebloan languages: *Tiwa* (spoken at Taos, Isleta, Picuris, and Sandia), *Towa* (Jemez), *Tewa* (Santa Clara, San Ildefonso, San Juan, Pojoaque, Nambe, and Tesuque), *Keres* (Cochiti, Santo Domingo, San Felipe, Zia, Santa Ana, Acoma, and Laguna), and *Zuni* (at Zuni).

The Pueblo peoples, unlike most of the more than 550 Indian tribes recognized by the U.S. government, have been living on the same lands they were living on when Europeans arrived. These people were never moved off their lands to distant reservations. When asked how long they've been in this area, some Pueblo elders will reply, "forever." Their enduring presence, as well as that of the Navajo and Apache people, is one of several features making New Mexico unique among her 49 sister-states.

At the bottom of the hill to your right is a sign for the village of **Tesuque**, confusingly named after the nearby pueblo. On the return trip you may want to take the time to visit this small New Mexico hamlet which several celebrities now call home. The Shidoni Foundry with its galleries and sculpture gardens is also located here (see *Part Six: Return Possibilities*). From this sign it is another 2.2 miles to the entrance of the pueblo itself. A turnoff to the left at Billco Carpets leads 8/10 mile to the heart of Tesuque Pueblo, which has about 400 residents. The old pueblo lies among the cottonwood trees on the banks of the Tesuque River, just ten miles north of Santa Fe.

Tesuque is one of the six Tewa language-speaking pueblos whose ancestors settled along the Rio Grande and its tributaries. The people call their village *Te-Tsu-Geh* (Cottonwood Tree Place). The Spanish pronounced it Tesuque (*Tay-SOO-kay*).

These beautiful 17,000-acres that drew Tesuque ancestors for their farming potential now attract TV and film producers. The TV series *Earth 2* was made here, as have been films with western backgrounds. But Tesuque doesn't rely on Hollywood moguls for tribal capital; it also operates a gaming casino, as well as an RV campground with a pool.

Although Pueblo people have a long agrarian tradition, few tribal members farm today. Many make their living in Santa Fe, Española or Los Alamos. Some derive a good income from crafting fine pottery or jewelry. Should you see a micaceous clay sculpture of a Rain God or bowls that feature frogs or lizards, you've most likely come upon the work of a Tesuque artisan.

More recently, the **Camel Rock Gaming Center**, 1.5 miles up the highway, has become the main source of income and employment for tribal members. A 55,000-square-foot casino, partially financed through revenue collected from an older bingo hall, attracts those who want to try their luck at slot machines, bingo, poker, roulette and craps.

While Tesuque is the most conservative of the Tewa pueblos, some tribal members would nevertheless be pleased to pick you up in Santa Fe tonight and take you to the casino. The enterprise, which opened in September 1995, distributes its income to benefit the entire pueblo, and is not distributed to each member annually, as is the practice of tribes elsewhere in the United States.

The Tesuques not only welcome people today, they also welcomed a Spanish soldier who came to "Cottonwood Tree Place" in the 1500s. He described seeing a large village with many-storied buildings and said the people were friendly, offering corn and squash. This friendly attitude did not last; Spanish rule in the 17th century prohibited native religious practices and insisted on conversion to Catholicism. A policy of forced labor was nothing less than slavery. These harsh conditions led to the Pueblo Revolt, and Tesuque played an important role in this successful Indian rebellion.

On August 9, 1680 two young Tesuque runners were captured by Spanish authorities. They were carrying a knotted yucca rope, each knot representing a day. Every day a knot was to be untied until there were none left, and on that day the Indian attack was set to begin. The capture of the runners negated the surprise element in this plan. The following morning Friar Pio, who came to perform a Mass at Tesuque, was slain. These two events led to an uprising which actually began three days earlier than originally planned. Even today residents honor the Tesuque youths who struck the first blow for religious freedom: all administrative offices are closed on August 10.

Currently, the two-story buildings in Tesuque's plaza area are being renovated to authentically reflect the village as it existed in the 1880s. When completed, the plaza will again be a beautiful place for the Tesuque Turtle Dance on Christmas Day (see *Pueblo Events Calendar*).

Site 3: Camel Rock ❧ *A Natural Anomaly*

From the entrance to Tesuque Pueblo, head north 1.5 miles toward Camel Rock Gaming Center. Across from the casino is the rock for which it is named. Mother Nature sculpted this unmistakably camel-like sandstone formation. On your return trip, looking at it head-on, you may see something very different!

Site 4: Pojoaque Pueblo ❧ *A People Returned*

A little over four miles beyond Camel Rock, you come upon the commercial activities of a second Indian settlement, **Pojoaque Pueblo**. A smaller pueblo than Tesuque, Pojoaque (*Po-WAH-kay*) is the home of another Tewa-speaking people. In the Spanish pronunciation, *P'o Suwae Geh* (Place to Drink Water) became *Pojoaque*.

Legend has it the Tewas entered the world from a mythical place beneath a lake to the north of today's villages. The first to rise up was a male figure, a supernatural being described as the "son of the sun." It was he who taught the art of living to the Tewa people. In their oral history, the people of Pojoaque tell of cave-dwelling ancestors living at Mesa Verde and surrounding valleys (near the Four Corners area where Arizona, Colorado, Utah and New Mexico meet). They say their forebears began settling in the Rio Grande Valley in northern New Mexico about A.D. 1200. Archaeologists believe that years of drought and over-population may have caused their migration south.

Following the Pueblo Revolt and final return of the Spanish in 1693, the Tesuque people resisted the culture imposed by the Europeans. In contrast, Pojoaque Pueblo took on many Spanish attributes they considered useful. Both tribes embraced the Catholic faith while keeping their own religion. Pojoaque made extensive use of domesticated farm animals, and included a variety of new fruits and vegetables in their diet.

Over the centuries, Pueblo inhabitants of the region have suffered profound threats to their continuity as a people. Episodic droughts, disease, and uncontrollable infestations of agricultural pests such as grasshoppers, as well as attacks by nomadic bands of Navajos and Apaches, tested Pojoaque's and other pueblos' ability to endure.

The people of Pojoaque were on the verge of extinction in 1890 due to a smallpox epidemic. Surviving tribal members abandoned their 11,600-acre home. Then in the 1930s several original families returned. Over the past 60 years, the population has increased and the vitality of its people has been restored.

As you come down the hill you will see evidence of their energy. The Pojoaque commercial area boasts a long strip of businesses, some pueblo-owned, others leased. You'll find a visitor center and gift shop (a good restroom stop), a Native American restaurant, supermarket, drugstore, liquor store, automotive service center, and the tribal cultural center.

The **Poeh Cultural Center** is the prominent adobe building with a tower and two *hornos* (beehive-shaped, earthen ovens) in front. It sits in the midst of a cluster of retail stores. The completed center will reflect the Tewa people's pride in their heritage. The four-story building will feature a sun tower, traditional kitchen and garden. Classes in pottery-making, painting, silversmithing and carving— skills handed down from generation to generation—will be offered, and a research center and computer classes are planned. Sculpture from all the northern pueblos will be displayed. Windows will face sites sacred to the Pueblo culture: one directed to Chaco Canyon in northwestern New Mexico; another to Mesa Verde in southwestern

Colorado; others will face the mountain peaks that form the geographic boundaries of the Pueblo world. Skylights, aligned with the sun at the summer equinox and winter solstice, will serve as a solar calendar. Thus, seasonal shifts of sunlight will dance with shadows on the floor.

Behind the hills in back of the commercial buildings lies the old village of Pojoaque where some 250 tribal members live. On December 12, the Feast Day of Our Lady of Guadalupe is celebrated here. Visitors are welcome to attend this ceremony (see *Pueblo Events*).

You'll see a large sign for the **Cities of Gold Casino** at the end of the commercial center. Once an elementary school, the building has been converted into a 24-hour gambling casino. (*Note:* the speed limit drops down to 35 mph here.)

As the highway divides just past downtown Pojoaque, follow the signs for NM Highway 502 and Los Alamos. You'll now be heading west. Just after this turn, you'll see Pojoaque High School on your right. About 2.5 miles down the road is Pojoaque Elementary School on your left, and after another 2.5 miles you'll come to the entrance to San Ildefonso Pueblo.

On your right as you pass the elementary school, a sign tells you that you have left Pojoaque Pueblo. Arising ahead you see flat-topped, brown, beige and pink formations called *mesas* (from the Spanish word for table). Above these mesas are the **Jemez Mountains**, ranging up to 11,000 feet. They are named after a pueblo on the other side of the peaks.

The Jemez range is the result of intermittent volcanic activity that took place over the past 10 million years. About a million years ago two series of eruptions reshaped the landscape. Geologists estimate these eruptions discharged over 50 cubic *miles* of rock—well over 100-fold the quantity of material ejected by the eruption of Mt. St. Helens in Washington in 1980. Ash from the Jemez eruptions has been found in Iowa, Oklahoma and Texas.

The second eruptions in this region created one of the world's largest *calderas* (collapsed volcanoes), about 15 miles across. It is possible to drive into a part of the caldera via NM Highway 4 above Los Alamos; once there you will experience a beautiful and vast alpine valley surrounded by Jemez Mountain peaks. At dawn in the summer, you may hear the sounds of elk bugling across the broad valley.

Look to the top of the mesas straight ahead, where white buildings are set against a green forest background. They are part of the 2000-building complex of **Los Alamos National Laboratory** (LANL). The laboratory is the outgrowth of the Manhattan Project. During World War II, American and foreign scientists gathered here for a top-secret research program—to develop the atomic bombs subsequently dropped on Hiroshima and Nagasaki.

Today LANL is one of three national defense laboratories under the auspices of the Department of Energy (others are Sandia in Albuquerque and Lawrence Livermore in Northern California). LANL is the largest employer in northern New Mexico, with a workforce of about 11,000 employees. The end of the Cold War saw a reduction in the development of new weapons, resulting in many layoffs.

Los Alamos National Laboratory is still primarily involved in nuclear weapons work, but there's a fair amount of interesting non-defense research going on. Approximately 200 companies are working with LANL to either develop commercial applications from defense technologies, or to use the laboratory's state-of-the-art computers and equipment. One example of industry/laboratory cooperation is George Lukas' (of *Star Wars* fame) use of LANL computers to enhance visual effects for films. Another is the Walt Disney Company's adaptation of a laboratory technology (originally designed to locate mines after the Gulf War) to test the stress and safety of rides at its theme parks.

Stop 5: San Ildefonso Pueblo 🦌 *Home of a Legendary Potter*

A small sign announcing **San Ildefonso Pueblo** will appear on your right. The turnoff to the village is approximately two miles beyond the sign. Unlike Tesuque and Pojoaque pueblos, San Ildefonso uses the name of its Spanish patron saint, rather than its older Tewa name, *Po Woh Ge Oweenge* (Where the Water Cuts Down Through). This pueblo is larger than the two you have already passed; its land encompasses close to 26,200 acres, and its population in 1990 was some 600 people.

San Ildefonso residents say their ancestors came from the much-studied Anasazi community at Mesa Verde in Southwestern Colorado, now a national park. When that region was abandoned about A.D. 1200 it is believed the people migrated to the gentle slopes of the

Jemez Mountains, known as the **Pajarito** (*pa-ha-REE-toe*, meaning Little Bird) **Plateau**. Tsankawi and Tsirege, now ruins, were former homes of San Ildefonso ancestors on this plateau. Archaeologists assume that in the 1400s these people moved down from the plateau to the Rio Grande Valley and settled across the river from the current village. By the time the Spanish arrived in the area in the late 1500s, the people of San Ildefonso were living at the village you are about to visit.

Turn right off NM 502 at the sign for San Ildefonso Pueblo. As you drive into the village you will notice a mixture of architectural styles. Traditional pueblo adobe style predominates in both newly-stuccoed brown homes and a few older structures. Abandoned adobe buildings show mud bricks dissolving to the elements. Besides flat-roofed homes, you will see pitched metal roofs and a mobile home.

A large white sign welcomes you to San Ildefonso as you arrive in the old village area. The Pueblo culture has its own values and expectations. Please be sensitive to these differences, and respect restrictions about off-limits areas and picture-taking (see *Pueblo Etiquette*).

Across the dirt road to the right of the sign is the **San Ildefonso Visitor Center**, generally open from 8 a.m. to 5 p.m. except Sundays and holidays. Here you pay a $3 entrance fee and can purchase a camera permit for $5. Additional fees are charged for the use of video cameras, sketching and painting. You will receive a map of areas on the pueblo that you can visit, which include the **Maria Poveka Martinez Museum**, the large central plaza, a spectacular adobe church (open during services only) and several shops that sell pottery and jewelry.

Before leaving the visitor center, take a look at several small displays. San Ildefonso is renowned for its burnished "black-on-black" pottery. This style was developed early in the 20th century by Maria Poveka Martinez and her husband, Julian. Maria is perhaps the best known of all Indian potters.

She was born in the 1880s and died in 1980. During her lifetime, Maria created hundreds of beautiful pieces that elevated modern Pueblo pottery from a folk art to a fine art, where the talent and name of the artist is key in determining the value of a work. Encouraged by Edgar Lee Hewett, a major figure in Southwestern archaeology and first director of the Museum of New Mexico, Maria re-created the shapes of ancient black pots and began to sign her name (and often Julian's name) to each work. Designs were inspired by pottery shards that Julian brought home from what is now Bandelier National Monument, where he helped with archaeological excavations. As was traditional practice among Pueblo people, Maria, the woman, hand-shaped the pots, while Julian, the man, painted designs on them.

The black-on-black style is now used by many potters at the pueblo. It is created by smothering the pots with pulverized horse dung during the outdoor firing process. By eliminating oxygen, the natural clay color (usually red at San Ildefonso) turns black. Besides the display of Maria's work in the visitor center, the pueblo museum has more excellent examples of her pots. Museum hours are Monday through Friday, 8 a.m. to 4 p.m.

As you leave the visitor center take note of the two small hills to your left. At dawn on the morning of January 23 these hills become part of a scene of wonder for outsiders, and a sacred event for pueblo members. If you arrive early that morning and park your car in a distant field, the sound of drumming calls from far away. When you reach what is usually the parking lot outside the visitor center, a group of Pueblo men will be standing in a line beating on large drums made

of aspen or cottonwood. Looking above the two hills, the eastern sky is gaining light; it is not quite time for the sun's appearance. The throbbing rhythm of the drums keeps repeating, repeating … Soon you may begin to feel in tune with the rhythm, a rhythm not of your culture, but one that begins to feel universal as it draws you in. Suddenly you notice smoke rising between the two hills from a fire that is out of sight. Moments later antlers appear above each hill, followed by two lines of deer silhouetted against the eastern sky. The deer dancers, using sticks decorated with pine boughs for front legs, wend their way down the hills toward you. Pueblo members wait in a group, and as the deer dancers pass, some reach out to touch them; others toss a cornmeal offering at the feet of the dancers. The deer continue onto the plaza area where they disappear into a kiva. This procession, and the actual deer dance performed later in the morning, are said to be a traditional way of thanking the deer spirit for providing sustenance to the community.

Dances continue off and on all day, following a Catholic mass said in the church. This is the Feast Day for San Ildefonso (Saint Alphonsus), the patron saint of the pueblo. Feasting takes place, too. The women begin food preparation weeks in advance. On the day of the event they may serve as many as two hundred people in their homes. Traditional outdoor oven bread, chile stews, *posole* (a tasty concoction of hominy and meat), salads and desserts are among the dishes offered. Relatives and friends from nearby pueblos and throughout the country come for this occasion.

Feast Days are observed in each pueblo on the day honoring their patron saint. During the early 1600s, Franciscan missionaries assigned a patron saint to each pueblo. Religion as observed today in pueblo communities is a blend of Catholic rituals and traditional native practices. Feast Days are celebrated throughout the year in the different pueblos. Ritual dances, performed on Christmas, Easter, days honoring saints, and seasonal equinoxes and solstices, as well as at planting, hunting and harvesting time, are often open to the public (see *Calendar of Pueblo Events*). Photography is generally not permitted at Pueblo dances. One exception is at San Ildefonso Pueblo, where a $20 "personal use" permit for still cameras has become available in recent years. This practice at San Ildefonso might change, so contact the Visitor Center or Governor's Office in advance for current regulations, (505) 455-2273.

Now let's explore the village of San Ildefonso, either on foot or by car. Your map shows a short, circular route that takes you around the plaza. While surrounding mountains define the geographic perimeter of the Pueblo world, the plaza at its center is its heart. Here upon the dry desert earth, through prayer, ritual and dance, nature's beneficence is traditionally implored, season after season.

As you head down the road to the left of the welcome sign, you skirt one of the two plazas. You pass the old *kiva*, the round, windowless ceremonial building with the ladder extending out of the roof at top of the stairs. Kivas are private sanctuaries for male tribal members, rarely open to women, never open to non-tribal members. The plaza as well is off-limits, except when public ceremonies or dances are held. (In sharp contrast, visitors to Taos Pueblo park on the plaza—each village, an independent entity, has its own rules and regulations.)

Pueblo people tend to be circumspect about their native religion, perhaps in response to the memory of early Spanish repression. Unlike Evangelicals who pursue converts, they won't let you join their religious community even if you want to. In some pueblos, non-Indian spouses are excluded from certain ceremonies, even though they have adopted the Pueblo way of life. In a few rare instances, non-Indians have been invited to become honorary members of a pueblo.

The buildings around the plaza are traditional yet mostly one and two-storied. No longer visible are three and four story structures the Spanish reported seeing after visits in the 16th century. Today several of these buildings are shops where you can find black-on-black pottery, as well as other pottery styles and jewelry from this village and neighboring pueblos. Behind the houses on the west side of the plaza is the village church. This adobe church was built in the 1960s, replacing three former churches. The first mission church erected in 1617 was destroyed at the time of the Pueblo Revolt.

In this area you will also see a seniors center, tribal court and administrative building. The large administrative building off to the left of the church is the **Governor's Office**. The Martinez Museum is attached, and presents the process of pottery-making. Several prized pots by Maria are on exhibit.

The Spanish instituted a governmental system for the pueblos that included a governor, lieutenant governor and a fiscal officer. In the beginning, despite Spanish intentions, these officials were primarily ceremonial. *Caciques* (*ka-SEE-kays*), spiritual leaders, remained final authorities. In time, the newer officials have begun serving an important function as liaisons between the non-native world and the tribe. When Kevin Costner wanted to film part of *Wyatt Earp* at Santa Clara Pueblo, he needed the Pueblo governor's permission to do so.

The process of selecting a governor and other secular officials varies by pueblo. Some are elected by male tribal members; others are appointed by spiritual leaders. In 1620 the sovereign authority of the pueblos was recognized in the form of a gift, a cane with a silver head, presented by a representative of the Spanish king. This physical symbol acknowledged the power of the pueblo governor. The tradition was continued during the Mexican Period. Upon learning of this custom in 1864, Abraham Lincoln presented each governor with a signed cane, now referred to as the "Lincoln Canes." These canes, a source of great pride to the Pueblo people, are passed from an outgoing governor to his or her successor. In some pueblos the passing of the cane is done in a public ceremony (see *Calendar of Pueblo Events*).

Continue your loop tour of the pueblo by returning to the plaza through the large wooden gate at the right of the church. This gate was erected by a film crew for *Two Flags West*, a Glenn Ford western, shot in the 1950s. The pueblo elected to leave it standing after the filming was finished.

After passing through this gate you cross the broad plaza, on a road that divides it into two. The two parts are now called the north and south plazas. Earlier in this century, a dispute arose among the inhabitants of this pueblo about which ceremonies were to be considered religious requiring participation, and which were to be considered secular and voluntary. Unable to agree, the village then separated into two groups called *moieties*, one associated with the north plaza and winter and the other with the south plaza and summer. On days when dances are open to the public, members affiliated with each plaza generally take turns dancing.

As you drive on the road across the plaza, you can't miss the enormous cottonwood tree towering over the grounds of the pueblo. The exact age of this magnificent specimen is not known, but its unforgettable presence has been documented in early 20th century photographs. You may have noticed several *hornos*—squat, earthen, beehive-shaped ovens near the village buildings. These communal ovens are not used for firing pottery but for baking bread, pies and cookies, especially for important festivities. During a recent spring visit to San Ildefonso, a resident remarked that the women would be firing up the hornos soon to bake the pies for a school graduation. She pointed to one horno, saying that it was a 25-pie horno, and indicated that a larger one nearby, was a 50-pie oven.

On the other side of the plaza is a cluster of shops: on the left is the shop of **Elvis Torres**, straight ahead is the shop of **Juan Tafoya**, and on the right is **Sunbeam Indian Arts**, where the works of Barbara Gonzalez, the granddaughter of Maria Martinez, are featured. These establishments are usually open from about 10 a.m. to about 5 p.m. They offer excellent examples of Pueblo craftsmanship, as well as good conversation with the artists/owners who are often there. Turn to your right at the stop sign to head back to the visitor center. On your right you'll see an abandoned adobe structure with an exposed traditional dirt roof with grass growing from it—considered a fine roof in an earlier period.

When you're ready to leave San Ildefonso, retrace your route past the visitor center and you will soon be back to the highway. Along the way you can visit **Babbitt's Cottonwood Trading Post**. Follow the signs. This shop is run much like the trading posts of yore, and sits on land purchased in 1912, one of the last sales of pueblo property to outsiders. Babbitt's carries a fine selection of Pueblo and Navajo goods, purchased directly from the artisans who make them. The trading post is open daily from 9 a.m. to 5:30 p.m., except Sundays.

Site 6: Otowi Bridge ❧ *Linking Antiquity and Nuclear Science*

Return to NM 502, turn right and continue west for about a mile. You will see a line of large deciduous trees ahead. In the Southwest this means water—in this case the "big water" or **Rio Grande**. To one visitor the Rio here seemed like the *Rio Pequeño* rather than Rio Grande, for only in spring does it usually fill its banks. However, it has long been the lifeblood of this area. Starting among the San Juan Mountains of southern Colorado, the Rio Grande flows due south, more or less carving the state of New Mexico in two. When the river leaves New Mexico to the south near El Paso, it curves to the southeast where it continues into the Gulf of Mexico. Beyond El Paso the river becomes the international border between the United

States and Mexico, a segment made famous both by Hollywood movies and news documentaries on illegal immigration. But for New Mexicans through the centuries, the Rio Grande has been the main source of precious water required for the crops that have supported Pueblo, Spanish and Anglo-American farmers alike.

Most pueblo villages are situated along the Rio Grande and its tributaries. Early in the 19th century, European travelers called the river "the Nile of the Southwest," for it overflowed its banks each spring as mountain snows melted. Then it receded, depositing rich minerals ideal for farming. The seasonal occurrence of flooding ceased when the U.S. Army Corps of Engineers built dams along the Rio Grande.

The suspension bridge just south of the highway spanning the Rio Grande is **Otowi Bridge** (Tewa for "A Place Where the Water Makes a Noise"). It is also the name of a former pueblo a few miles to the west. This old bridge to the left of the modern one was constructed in 1943 to bring in heavy construction materials for the Manhattan Project in Los Alamos. In 1945 the world's first atomic bomb rumbled across it on its way to detonation at Trinity Site in southern New Mexico.

Otowi Bridge was made famous in Peggy Pound Church's *The House at Otowi Bridge*. Her book tells the story of Edith Warner, a Baptist minister's daughter, who came out West upon orders from her doctor. The adobe home she rented from Maria and Julian Martinez was situated near a stop on the narrow-gauge railroad called the **Chile Line**. This New Mexico branch of the Denver and Rio Grande Railroad commenced at Alamosa, Colorado and ended in Santa Fe. The Chile Line ran from 1880 to 1941. Warner was hired as station mistress at this site by the Los Alamos Ranch School for boys, which was situated on a mesa top high above. She collected supplies destined for the school, and awaited twice-weekly pickups by school representatives.

Warner became friends with her Pueblo neighbors and was invited to their ceremonies and into their homes. To help support herself she opened a tea room. Her soon-to-be-famous chocolate cake drew travelers to her remote establishment. Among those who stopped in for a treat was Robert Oppenheimer, who happened to be backpacking in the area.

Dr. Oppenheimer returned in 1942 to oversee the Manhattan Project, the super-secret crash program to build the atomic bomb. A once far-away setting for a boys school was transformed almost overnight into a sprawling town and research and development facility.

Within the confines of Warner's tiny tea room, two diverse cultures mingled: a Pueblo people rooted in their past, and world-famous scientists determined to reshape the future. When Edith Warner died in 1951, she was laid to rest in an unmarked grave near San Ildefonso Pueblo. Above the bare earth where she was buried, broken pottery shards were sprinkled in an ancient Native American tradition.

The life of Edith Warner, an independent woman living in an isolated area of the Southwest, inspired noted author Frank Waters to write *Woman at Otowi Crossing*. Waters' book in turn served as inspiration for an opera of the same name by Stephen Paulus, which premiered in St. Louis in 1995. Santa Feans at the performance say the audience was on its feet with delight.

On crossing the Rio Grande you are at the lowest elevation of your journey, about 5550 feet above sea level. Continue on NM 502 up the hill for 1.5 miles and turn right onto NM 30. From here your journey continues on to Santa Clara Pueblo land and Puye Cliff Dwellings.

PUYE TO POSHUOUINGE

In the Footsteps of the Ancient Ones

The wind and rain come to clean,
The time of their working is past.
Now sleep the Old Ones...
Now sleep the Old Ones...

—Tewa (author unknown)

✪ **Approximate Time: 1¾ hours, includes Poshuouinge but not Puye**
(allow 3 hours with a visit to Puye)
Approximate Distance: 27 miles (43 miles with visit to Puye)

IN A CAVE AND CLIFF-TOP CITY just up the road, an ancient people took refuge from the wind and rain. There, almost 800 years ago, a community thrived. The people hunted, raised corn, beans and squash, made pottery and tools, wove cloth, and patiently pecked images (petroglyphs) into the rocks. After 300 years at this site they moved on—taking with them their spiritual practices which live on in the prayer-dance dramas of their Pueblo descendants.

Site 1: Black Mesa ⇜ *Home of Giants*

From your turn onto NM 30 drive five miles to a left-hand turn toward Puye Cliffs. Enroute as you head northeast, a striking rock formation rises directly in front of you. This is **Black Mesa**, a volcanic plug, the innards of an erupted volcano whose outer shell has eroded. During thunderstorms Black Mesa's appearance becomes particularly dark and threatening—hence its name. In Tewa, it is called *Tunyo* (*TOON-yo*), a spot alone. This unusual outcropping is sacred to both Santa Clara and San Ildefonso pueblos. According to one Santa Clara tour guide, so sacred is Tunyo that only with permission from village elders may tribal members scale it. It is also said to be the home of a giant who Tewa mothers say will punish naughty children.

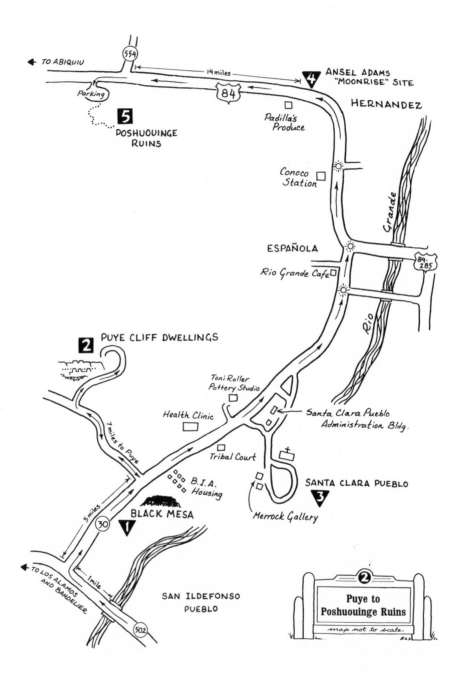

TO ABIQUIU

554

14 miles

84

Parking

5

POSHUOUINGE
RUINS

Padilla's
Produce

Conoco
Station

ANSEL ADAMS
"MOONRISE" SITE

4

HERNANDEZ

Grande

ESPAÑOLA

Rio Grande Cafe

84
285

Rio

PUYE CLIFF DWELLINGS

2

Toni Roller
Pottery Studio

7 miles to Puye

Health Clinic

Tribal Court

B.I.A.
Housing

5 miles

30

BLACK MESA

1

Santa Clara Pueblo
Administration Bldg.

SANTA CLARA PUEBLO

3

Merrock Gallery

TO LOS ALAMOS
AND BANDELIER

1 mile

502

SAN ILDEFONSO
PUEBLO

2

**Puye to
Poshuouinge Ruins**

map not to scale

The Spanish, having heard this story, named the area *Los Gigantes* (the giants).

This mesa played a part in the Pueblo Revolt of 1680. After Don Diego de Vargas reconquered New Mexico, re-establishing Spanish rule in Santa Fe, there were a few uprisings among some of the pueblos in the years that followed. In 1694, the peoples of Tesuque, Santa Clara and San Ildefonso Pueblos rebelled and abandoned their villages, taking a defensive position atop Black Mesa. De Vargas and his soldiers arrived and lay siege at the foot of the mesa. Short on food and ammunition, the Spanish eventually had to retreat to Santa Fe, handing the Indians a victory.

Two years later, according to local lore, San Ildefonso rose in rebellion a second time. Once again the people took refuge on Black Mesa. This time De Vargas came prepared for a long siege. Legends about this historical event tell of Indian women cutting their long black hair and tying it into ropes. The ropes were then used to haul food supplied by Indian allies to the mesa top. But, so the story goes, Spanish soldiers discovered these friends and killed them. Finally the Indians surrendered, and although most then returned to their village, some warriors reportedly jumped to their death rather than submit to Spanish authority.

As you get closer to Black Mesa, the road bends to the left and you pass the mesa on your right. From this vantage point the formation truly does "stand alone," as the Tewas say. A little further down the road on your right you will see a brown sign announcing the home of the Santa Clara people, and telling you that on this land you are subject to all tribal and federal laws. Continue on NM 30 for about one mile to a left-hand turnoff for Puye Cliffs Dwellings.

You are now at a decision point. Seven miles and about 15 minutes up this road is Puye (commonly pronounced *"poo-yay,"* although Tessie Naranjo, Director of Cultural Preservation at Santa Clara Pueblo, says Tewa speakers pronounce it *"poo-jay"*). Administered by Santa Clara Pueblo, Puye comprises the most complete Anasazi ruins on this trip, and includes cave dwellings, cliff houses, petroglyphs, kivas, and a large excavated village. We suggest a stop at *either* Puye Cliffs *or* Poshuouinge—an unexcavated, large, but less-diverse Anasazi site right along the main route (*see Stop 5*).

Stop 2: Puye Cliff Dwellings ૨ᐩ

Rocks Speak of a Vanished People

Anasazi? What is the meaning of this unusual word that people often trip over when they first encounter it? Derived from the Navajo language, it is most commonly considered to mean "the ancient ones." However, since no such word exists in Navajo today, you may also see it translated as "enemy ancestors." Both translations make sense in light of the relatively recent arrival of the Navajo into a Southwest already settled by the Pueblo Indians.

A generally accepted theory among archaeologists is that the Navajo and their sister people, the Apache, drifted down from the north sometime in the two or three centuries before the Spanish arrived in 1540. Being nomadic hunters, they must have been impressed by the Pueblo culture they encountered, particularly by the permanent villages inhabited by farmers who lived a lifestyle so different from their own. These new migrants would have also come upon abandoned towns of the forebearers (ancient ones) of the Pueblo people they met. The Navajo often raided pueblos, so it's logical that they thought of the Anasazi as their enemies' ancestors.

There's another possibility. While visiting the Navajo sacred area at Canyon de Chelly in northeastern Arizona, we encountered a Navajo ranger working there who put together two Navajo words and said they sounded close to "anasazi." He said they meant "skinny enemy."

If you elect to make the journey to Puye, immediately you will see a sign telling you that parking along the road is prohibited for 15 miles. Santa Clara Pueblo does not permit exploration of its land. The only stops allowed along this road are at Puye Cliff Dwellings, seven miles up the road, or at **Santa Clara Canyon**, a recreation area 15 miles from the turnoff from NM 30.

The road takes you from the Rio Grande Valley at an elevation of about 5600 feet to 6800 feet above sea level, up on the Pajarito Plateau at Puye. You will notice several changes in vegetation as you ascend. From a few small juniper trees the landscape fills with larger and increasing numbers of both piñon pine and juniper. As you climb still higher, ponderosa pines appear to the right. These tall evergreens, with long needles and very straight trunks, are used for vigas, the round roof beams seen throughout northern New Mexico. Ponderosas thicken as you get higher and approach Puye Cliffs. The long mesa comes into view on the right, about six miles after your turnoff from NM 30. Along the roadside, western and mountain bluebirds are often perched on electric wires and in the evergreens.

The turn into **Puye Cliff Dwellings** is on your right. Cave openings can be spotted from this distance. Quickly you come to the entrance station. Admission is $5 for adults and $4 for seniors and children. There is no additional fee for still cameras, but there's a $15 charge for the use of video cameras.

The ranger at the station will give you a pamphlet on Puye (ask for it if one isn't offered) and answer your questions. Occasionally in the summer, a teenager from the pueblo is on hand to give a guided tour; ask the ranger about availability and cost.

The parking lot is one-quarter mile ahead. Park and prepare for an adventure back in time to the caves above you. The walk to the caves is only about one-half mile, but before leaving your car make sure you have comfortable walking shoes, hat, sunglasses, water and (if appropriate) raingear, since it may be a while before you return.

As you are about to step into the footsteps of the ancient ones, try to imagine people living here over seven centuries ago. Archaeologists and Native Americans have pieced together the clues left behind to give us some understanding of their life.

Openings in the rock first provided shelter from wind and weather. When the rains came and the snows melted, the people collected water from mountain runoffs, funneling it through canals to their farm fields.

With bow and arrow and spear, they hunted deer, elk, long-horned sheep, raccoon, and bear. Squirrel, rabbit and wild turkey were occasional additions to their diet. The Anasazi staples of corn, beans, squash and animal protein had to be supplemented by yucca fruits and seeds, prickly pear, beeweed, piñon nuts, wild plums and choke cherries.

Turkey feathers were used for robes and blankets and also for ceremonial purposes, as they are today. The Puye people turned to wild plants for medicine, baskets, rope, and shampoo. Dyes were extracted from flowers and rocks for decorating pottery. With wood and stone tools, they felled trees for roof beams and firewood.

Under these circumstances, archaeologists estimate an average lifespan of about 40 years. A total of 230 burials have been found at Puye, with 171 individuals in burial mounds northeast of the village on top of the mesa. In contrast, infants were found buried under fire pits in their homes. With many of the remains, fragments of fabric, small corn cobs, wooden flutes, and prayer sticks were discovered. Skeletal analysis indicates some suffered from arthritis, deadly intestinal parasites (such as whip worms), tuberculosis, and venereal syphilis.

While disagreements as to interpretation of findings persist among archaeologists, all agree it took courage, ingenuity, physical stamina and skill, as well as keen observation, to survive in the Anasazi world.

Santa Clarans say Puye means "pueblo where the rabbits gather," though we've not seen a jackrabbit or cottontail here.

A cave-dwelling culture lived at the mesa from approximately A.D. 1200 to A.D. 1500. In time, rock houses—known as *talus* houses—were built against the cliff face of the mesa, with caves used as back rooms. By about 1300 a large free-standing village was beginning to take shape on the top of the mesa to accommodate the increasing population. Santa Clarans say that at one time over 1500 people lived alongside or on this mesa. Some archaeologists estimate 2000. Caves stretch for over a mile on the mesa's south and west flanks; in some places you'll see these caves are on two distinct levels.

Now let's be explorers! Head up the steps and you will first notice a building with a sign that says **Harvey House**—a former restaurant. Was one of the famous Harvey hostelries here in Anasazi times? We don't think so! The Fred Harvey Company, to complement its hotel and restaurant business, operated tours to Indian country in conjunction with the Santa Fe Railroad. Their Indian Detours enterprise took tourists to the pueblos from Santa Fe, and this building was used as a lunch stop. Restrooms will be found to your right once you have reached the patio behind the Harvey House.

Walk to the top of the stairs and follow the rough, cobbled path toward the mesa. As you climb, you will come into close company with piñon and juniper trees. The trail heads slightly off to the left. When it makes a sharp turn to the right, look just beyond the large rock in front of you at the turn to the rock face behind it. Here is your first *petroglyph*, depicting an Indian hunter with feathered headdress, holding a bow and arrow. If you're short, you may need to get on tiptoes, or carefully stand on the rocks lining the trail.

Continue up to the cave openings at the end of the path. If you begin to feel that you can't make it much further, slow down and breathe deeply. (Remember, you're at almost 7000 feet; if you come from lower climes, it usually takes a number of days before your body adjusts to the lower oxygen supply here—almost 25 percent *less* than at sea level. You may be surprised how quickly your body forces you to take a break.)

At the end of the trail the fun begins! Before you are caves, or *cavates*, as they are called by archaeologists. Notice the rock of the cave walls. This is *tuff*—not "tough"—for it is soft, light rock formed from volcanic ash which has solidified. You are feeling a product from volcanic eruptions that formed this plateau over a million years ago.

Inside the caves are smoke-blackened ceilings, remnants of mud plaster used to hold the crumbly tuff, and small man-made compart-ments. The soft tuff allowed the Indians to enlarge caves easily and make these cubbyholes. What these little openings were used for is unknown. The crumbly characteristic of tuff, combined with rain and melting snow seeping into this porous rock, likely caused some caves to collapse. Personal safety was probably a constant concern, yet here the inhabitants slept, ate and performed the daily tasks of their agriculturally-based lifestyle.

Above the caves at the head of the trail, you'll encounter other petroglyphs, depicting an animal and concentric circles. How did they get up there? What do they mean? To find the answer to the first question, face the cliffs and turn left. Follow the path to the talus (rock) houses that you see built off the cliff face. These few houses have been reconstructed as examples of the numerous similar dwellings that once lined these cliffs. Evidence is clear: the horizontal rows of holes in the rock once held the ends of roof beams of talus houses.

Many more petroglyphs can be found to the right, above these rebuilt rock dwellings. From here it's easy to imagine people standing on the roofs of the houses and creating the pictures above you.

What do petroglyphs mean? Some authors call them "rock art," but did the Anasazi think of these creations as art? We may never know for certain, because the ancient ones left no written language. Western civilization's concept of art today may be very different from how these people regarded these expressions of human creativity.

Possibly the best source for an explanation are the insights of descendants of these ancient Pueblo people. Amadeo Shije, Governor of Zia Pueblo, wrote about petroglyphs in a piece that appeared in the *Albuquerque Journal*. He spoke out for the need to protect the rock carvings at Petroglyphs National Monument near Albuquerque in the face of a proposed highway through the park. He said that "Pueblo ancestors 'wrote' down the visions and experiences they felt." Petroglyph sites, such as Puye, are considered sacred by all Pueblo people.

While observing the rock images here, look for two other noteworthy petroglyphs. High above the right corner of the talus houses you will see a set of concentric circles with holes on the lines of these circles. A Santa Clara native told us that this symbol was used as a calendar. Scholars have discovered a number of archaeoastronomical glyphs like these in the region. The guess is that Native Americans of the Southwest observed movements of the sun and moon and the changing of seasons to schedule their plantings and perpetuate their culture. One well-known example of rock drawings relating to heavenly events is the so-called Sun Dagger on Fajada Butte at Chaco Canyon National Historical Park. Another archaeo-astronomy site is at Chimney Rock in southern Colorado where a certain full moon shines through the stone "chimneys" every 18 years.

A second image often depicted in the Anasazi world can be seen if you stand away from the talus houses and look on the wall just above the roofs. There you can make out the fading image of *Avanyu*, the water serpent. You may have seen this image of a plumed serpent painted or carved on pottery made in New Mexico. Avanyu is said to be the spirit that governs all terrestrial water. Today some believe this symbol marked a nearby spring or other water source. A member of San Ildefonso Pueblo told us that Avanyu comes with summer rain clouds. And if the people have the right spirit in their minds and hearts when they dance, the rains will come to nourish their sacred corn.

Head back to the trail and decide whether to climb the ladder or ride your steel horse. Ahead is an enormous ladder which provides access to caves on a second level and the mesa top. You can get to the large excavated village on top either by ladder and trail, or by car on a one-mile drive. The ladder is the more picturesque route. However, the trail above the ladder is steep and you have to come back down the ladder, a feat many people find daunting. Even for non-ladder climbers, a great "Kodak moment" is at hand. Climb up just three or four rungs and have someone take your photograph from down low, to include the huge ladder, cliffs and sky. (Your home-bound relatives will be impressed!)

Now you're set to visit the large free-standing village on the top of the mesa. Either use the ladder and trail above, or retrace your steps to the parking lot, and take your gasoline-powered steed on the road that exits from the parking area toward the east. Archaeologists have found over a dozen ancient trails from the cave area to the top. *Imagine* yourself climbing on those pathways up these walls, using hand-and-foot holds—but please don't try this.

When you're on top, you will see the remains of ground-floor walls, part of one large village. This settlement was the earliest excavated site on the Pajarito Plateau. The work began in 1907. Diggers uncovered four massive blocks of attached rooms surrounding a large plaza. Although archaeologists have thoroughly excavated the rooms on the east, south, and part of the west sides of the village, they have not reconstructed rooms. However, they stabilized portions of the walls that remained after almost 400 years of weathering and blowing earth had covered the dwellings. It is believed that as Puye's population grew, many of its structures had two or even three stories.

The plaza before you was the center of social activity for the Puye people, just as today the plaza is the center of social life for Pueblo Indians. Women ground corn here using stone *manos* and *metates*. Using stone scrapers, the men prepared animal hides for winter clothing. Here children played, gossip was whispered, and public ceremonies united Puye inhabitants into a community.

If you were standing just outside the village in the 1400s, you would have seen men working in fields of corn, beans and squash. Water to nourish these plants is said to have come from a spring nearby on the mesa. The canyon bottoms below were also used for raising additional crops.

Don't miss the large kiva on the east side of the village at the edge of the mesa-top parking area. This round, subterranean spiritual chamber has an entrance on the roof leading to a large room below ground. Notice an opening on ground level to the east. It's a ventilator shaft which allowed fresh air to enter the kiva to feed a sacred fire. When the kiva was in use, smoke could be seen coming from the roof entrance. Some believe those entering this holy place were purified by the rising smoke as they climbed below.

On the southwest side of the plaza you'll find a two-story structure that's an exception in that it has been rebuilt. A sign outside says *Community House*. You've probably noticed how small the rooms are—no double beds here! Anasazi villagers were an outdoor people, probably sleeping on rooftops when the weather permitted. The rooms were only about five feet high. You might think that low ceilings suggest short people. However, a National Park Service source says that male Anasazis in this area averaged five feet three to four inches in stature and the women about five feet—about the same height as their contemporaries in Europe. An explanation for small rooms with small doorways is that they retain heat better in winter.

It is believed Puye was abandoned in the late 1500s. Santa Clarans speak of a drought that dried up local springs, forcing their ancestors to settle below the mesa along the Rio Grande. Climatologists say based on tree-ring data, this drought was the worst in a thousand years. Archaeologists also speculate that after hundreds of years of occupation nearby wood resources were depleted. This probably compelled the inhabitants to travel far for firewood for cooking, heating and lighting. Other possible explanations for abandonment include enemy attack, disease, and internal feuding.

The view from the edge of the mesa is awe-inspiring. To the east lie the Sangre de Cristos in full splendor. Follow these mountains to the south where they become small hills; right in front of those hills is Santa Fe. Due south, the large round mountain you see is **Sandia Peak**, above Albuquerque. As you look westward into the Jemez Mountains, you may be able to pick out the ski trails of the **Pajarito Ski Area**, above Los Alamos. From the other side of the mesa, the mountains above Taos can be seen—stunning when snow-covered. These peaks are the highest in New Mexico, with Mt. Wheeler reaching 13,161 feet.

Once you have explored the village and savored the vistas, return to your car or retrace your tracks down the mesa. (Take care coming down the ladder.) Exit the park by turning left after the entrance station and drive the seven miles back to NM 30. When you reach the highway, turn left and head toward Santa Clara Pueblo (about two miles down the road) and the town of Española.

Site 3: Santa Clara Pueblo 🐚 *Adobe Homes and Pickup Trucks*

You are heading toward the main residential area of Santa Clara Pueblo on your way to O'Keeffe country. It's an interesting visit and pottery connoisseurs and collectors need look no further for the highly-valued black pots made by the Santa Clara people.

As you drive down the road, you may be surprised to see rows of identical homes on the right. This "suburb," about a mile before the older main village, is not particularly distinctive or Southwestern in style. It is the fruit of funding by the U.S. Bureau of Indian Affairs. A little further on the left you will pass the pueblo's baseball diamond followed by a modern health clinic. The government's Indian Health Service provides health care to Indian tribes across the country.

Across the road from the clinic, you'll see two older buildings. A sign indicates the pueblo's tribal court and rehabilitation center. New Mexico's pueblos are dry by tribal law, but alcohol is readily available in nearby towns. Drug and alcohol abuse exists at the pueblos, just as it does in other communities in New Mexico and throughout the United States.

Less than a mile further on your left is a red sign announcing the **Toni Roller Pottery Studio** (753-3003). Just a short quarter mile down the bumpy dirt road you will discover some of the best examples of Santa Clara black pottery. Toni Roller is the daughter of Margaret Tafoya, Santa Clara's preeminent potter. If you are fortunate, either Toni or one of her sons will be working pots and will describe the lengthy and complex process required to turn clay into ceramic vessels. Mrs. Roller and her son Cliff were invited to demonstrate their pottery-making during President Clinton's inaugural celebration in Washington—only one of two Indian families so honored.

Roller pots are easily recognized by their extremely clean carving. Carving, or incising of wares prior to their firing in outdoor pit fires, is a well-known feature of Santa Clara pots. Look for traditional Pueblo symbols on the clayware—Avanyu the plumed serpent and the bear paw. Ask if any of the family pots on display were created by Margaret Tafoya, the matriarch of the family, who is now in her 90s. Famous for crafting enormous pots that are extremely difficult to make, she was still producing a few pieces at the time of this writing.

Down through the ages, pottery has played a significant role in the lives of most indigenous people. For centuries vessels were made for storage, cooking, carrying water and ceremonial purposes. A variety of clays were used. At the turn of the 20th century, when a tourist market developed, the production of pottery changed. Visitors and collectors became prime consumers. The pots, at first large, became smaller (easier to carry home), and design was emphasized. Hand-shaped by Pueblo potters, these much-desired pieces have become an art form, rewarding some artists with a handsome income.

When you leave the Roller Studio, return to NM 30 and continue on your journey with a left turn. If you wish to visit the old area of the pueblo, make an immediate right at the sign indicating the pueblo entrance (1/10 mile). Santa Clara Pueblo does not have as large a plaza as the one you saw at San Ildefonso. However, in this plaza area are several shops with excellent pottery and jewelry from Santa Clara and other pueblos.

To get to the plaza, follow the entrance sign to the tee and turn right. (If you want to use a video or still camera or sketch, you'll need to visit the Tourism Office for a permit; turn left at the tee and proceed across the bridge to the large administrative building on the left just after the senior center. The office is only open on weekdays— please don't take pictures on weekends.) As you head toward the plaza, continue directly ahead. A left turn brings you to the front of the pueblo church (it's open only for services).

By going straight instead, you will come to a small open area surrounded by adobe structures. Two of the buildings in front of you are fine galleries—the **Merrock Gallery** sign is a landmark that lets you know you've reached the plaza.

In this small open space, and several others nearby, traditional dances are performed by Santa Clarans. August 12 is the major feast day for the village, honoring their patroness Saint Clare. On this day in a recent (and typical) year, three different groups performed a Corn Dance and a fourth group did a Rainbow Dance. The church area was bustling with numerous craftsmen from the Pueblo world, and the air was filled with the aroma of spicy Indian food—quite a contrast to the quiet and stillness you find on non-ceremonial days.

Santa Clarans also speak Tewa. *Kha P'o* ("Singing Water" or "Valley of the Wild Roses") is the Tewa name of the village. This pueblo is the largest of the four that you have passed on your route. It sits on 47,000 acres and has a population of about 1500. Farming, although not as prevalent as in times past, is still practiced near the Rio Grande. Ranching is common on the vast drier lands away from the river. (You may have encountered cattle on the road to Puye—open range grazing is the rule here.) Many residents are artists. Others travel to jobs in Los Alamos, Española and Santa Fe.

The modern history of Santa Clara includes a unique event. Between 1894 and 1934 intense factionalism developed at the pueblo. At issue was whether participation in ceremonials should be obligatory, and whether secular activities should be distinct from religious activities. This difference of opinion split the village. Four factions arose, and their inability to reach a compromise led to federal government intervention. In 1934 the local U.S. Indian Service arbitrated the creation of the first Pueblo constitution. Pueblo members approved the constitution which provided for an elective form of government and a resolution to these long-standing disputes.

Let's continue the journey. Make your way back to NM 30 by retracing your incoming route. Or take one of several roads that will get you there and allow further glimpses of the pueblo. Turn right onto NM 30. In less than a mile you'll leave pueblo land behind. A green sign for the town of Española will be your next landmark.

Your route takes you along the west side of this community where about 15,000 people live. (If you're hungry and aren't picnicking today, see *Part Six* and the *Appendix* for recommended restaurants.) Continue to the second traffic light, where you turn left onto US 84/285—the same highway you took departing Santa Fe. As you proceed, you pass Española's City Hall and the campus of **Northern New Mexico Community College** on the right. Very soon (1.3 miles from the turn at the light) you will come to a traffic light with a Conoco station on your left. Check your odometer, for we refer to mileage in the upcoming segment. You are now on your way to Abiquiu and O'Keeffe Country, about twenty miles up this road.

Site 4: Hernandez and Ansel Adams ❧ *"It's a stunning thing."*

As you make your way northwestward, you might easily miss Hernandez, a small village with a long history. Typical of many Hispanic villages, Hernandez has achieved a widespread familiarity through the photographic genius of Ansel Adams.

Moonrise, Hernandez, New Mexico, 1941 is the name of a celebrated work by Adams. With absolute clarity of focus, the photograph depicts a black velvet night sky, serving as the back-drop for a three-quarter moon. In this picture, which Adams himself described as one of his best, a silver light plays over a graveyard, church, cluster of homes, and surrounding mountains. The photograph captures the silence and solemnity of the moment, the comfort of community, and the temporality of our existence. Adams took only two exposures of this scene, but he made numerous prints. These prints often appear in retrospective exhibits, Ansel Adams calendars, and anthologies of his work.

Should you want to locate the actual site where the photograph was taken, here are the directions: From the traffic light at the Conoco station on the outskirts of Española, drive almost four miles to a sign indicating Hernandez Elementary School. Cross over an arroyo and pass the abandoned gas station (2/10 mile further). On your right (1/10 mile more), look for the adobe church and graveyard shown in the photograph, which today sit behind a white trailer beside the road. You are now passing the same vantage point the photographer used to take his picture. Things have changed, haven't they? Should you decide to stop on the side of this busy highway, we strongly encourage you to remain in your car as some Hernandez residents object to trespassers.

Care to view a print of the original Adams photograph? Check the **Fine Arts Museum** in Santa Fe, where one is sometimes on display. If unsuccessful there, the **Historic Artistic Patrimony and Archives**, a museum of the Catholic Archdiocese of Santa Fe, located at 223 Cathedral Place, has a print of this work on permanent exhibit (for hours: 983-3811).

Ansel Adams was one of the greatest photographic artists of this century. He ranks with such notable photographers as Paul Strand, Edward Weston, Dorothea Lange, and Alfred Stieglitz. The tall, thin-bearded photographer became part of a small coterie of art and literary friends Georgia O'Keeffe made in New Mexico. Adams and O'Keeffe met in Mabel Dodge Lujan's living room in Taos in 1929. Mabel Dodge Lujan was a patron of art and literature who drew many of America's most illustrious painters, writers and photographers to her salon in northern New Mexico.

Miss O'Keeffe admired Adams and often lent him her Ford to go traipsing around the countryside. They traveled together to Yosemite National Park, a special place for Adams, who returned there every year of his adult life. They shared a long, close friendship and a love of the landscape and nature.

Adams died in 1984 at the age of 82. During his lifetime he served as a director of the Sierra Club, taught workshops, wrote books, ran a gallery, developed new photographic techniques, and participated in over 500 museum exhibits. He lobbied to preserve land as national parks and was awarded the Medal of Freedom by President Jimmy Carter. Through his unforgettable pictures, including his famous image of Hernandez, he left the world a wonderful legacy.

On with the journey. Before you go too far you should see Padilla's fruit stand (1/10 mile on your left). Here in the fall you'll find fresh roasted green chile, local apples and other farm produce. If you're lucky you'll also find Mrs. Padilla who may regale you with local lore about Ansel Adams.

Your next Stop is about 15 miles up the road. As Hernandez fades in the distance, open fields come into view. The **Rio Chama**, not in sight at first, flows behind the large cottonwood trees to your right. The Chama, a tributary of the Rio Grande, is the irrigation source for crops grown all along the **Chama River Valley** you are now driving through.

This stretch of the route is a good place to look for birds common throughout northern New Mexico. Most often seen are the *ravens*. You may not recognize these birds if you're not from the Rocky Mountain region. In the same family and similar in appearance to crows, these black birds are larger and have wedge-shaped tails, thus distinguishing themselves from their more ubiquitous cousins.

Ornithologists consider both ravens and crows to be among the smartest of our feathered friends. For instance, they have been known to cast seeds onto roadways to be cracked open by passing cars. Watch for their joyful comraderie and listen for their familiar and playful "caw!"

You may also sight a long-tailed bird that often flies in pairs or small groups. These are *magpies*, whose tails are as long their bodies. In flight, their striking white and black feathers catch your eye. Other birds you might see include *kestrels* on telephone wires, blue *piñon jays* dashing in and out of trees, and *hawks* and *turkey vultures* circling above.

Vegetation along the roadside for part of the year is fairly sparse. However, with sufficient rain in certain seasons, plants burst into color bringing life to the landscape. In summer you may see patches of *scarlet paintbrush*, a low-growing plant and member of the snapdragon family. Scarlet paintbrush was used by the Tewa people to prepare a red dye for deerskins. Liquid extracted from the whole plant was added to baths to soothe aches and pains.

Another medicinal plant common near northern New Mexico's roadways is gray-green *sagebrush*. While its toothed leaves are distinctive, it is most easily identified by its pungent, pleasant aroma.

In August and September, *wild sunflowers*, significantly smaller than their cousin the cultivated sunflower, dance along the roadside. With its dark center, this plant may remind you of a black-eyed Susan. Though small, the seeds of this flower were an important protein and mineral source for the Pueblo people. Its strong stems were used for bird snares and arrows.

From late August until heavy frost, silvery-green bushes close to the pavement explode with bright yellow blooms. This is *chamisa*, or rabbitbrush. Its blossoms produce a dye used for centuries by both Indians and Spanish. Medicinally, the Indians made a tea from chamisa to cure upset stomachs and as a gargle for sore throats. Amidst the yellows of the chamisa and sunflowers, you may see touches of purple and blue. The wild *purple aster* and the *blue cornflower* are common along the roadways of northern New Mexico in late summer and fall.

About 12 miles beyond Hernandez the hills begin to loom larger. Ahead on the right you will see **Monte Negro** (Black Mountain). On its flank nearest you is a rock formation that looks to some like a medieval city. Rock formations in New Mexico often invite you to use your imagination.

Stop 5: Poshuouinge 〰 *A Trail to Antiquity*

Once you have passed Monte Negro, start looking for NM 554 on your right, 14 miles from Padilla's fruit stand. Continue on US 84 for about 1¼ miles beyond that intersection and look for a small brown and white sign on your left announcing **Poshuouinge** (*po-shoe-o-WIN-gay*). Slow down or you might miss it! If you didn't stop at Puye Cliffs, but still wish to see an Anasazi ruin, turn left off the highway into the parking area just beside the road.

A narrow, winding, rock-strewn path, ascending one quarter mile from where you park, will take you to the unexcavated ruins of an Anasazi settlement built prior to A.D. 1400. Poshuouinge (Tewa for "village above muddy river") is on the mesa above the parking lot. It is believed to have been occupied until about A.D. 1500

Stone tracings suggest the architectural imprint of a large town with approximately 700 ground floor rooms, two plazas and a large kiva. To the east of the town lay farming fields central to the life of all Anasazi communities. Poshuouinge's main houseblock (apartment-like complex) is likely to have had a second story, and possibly some third floor rooms. With this floor plan, archaeologists estimate that over a thousand rooms once stood here. Not all rooms were lived in; many were used for storing crops.

Neighboring Tewa-speaking Pueblos, descendants of these Anasazi people, regard this ancestral site as a sacred place. The treeless mesa is rich in pottery shards of the black-on-white variety common to this area. Fascinating to find, they are a valuable part of the archeological record and are not to be moved under penalty of law. Changing the natural site of even a single shard destroys its "provenience," and therefore its significance to the understanding of the past.

As you walk on this sacred ground, you will see *snakeweed*, a low-growing plant plentiful in this locale. Green in spring, its bushy heads turn bright yellow in late summer. The people who lived here and their descendants used this plant to treat aches, eye disorders, and insect and rattlesnake bites.

Before returning to your car, continue on the path to the top of a nearby hill beyond a wooden rail fence. There you will come to a lean-to built by the Santa Fe National Forest. From here you'll see the outlines of the village and get a broad overview of the river valley below and Monte Negro beyond. This view is particularly lovely in the spring when the cottonwoods are greening, and stunning in early fall when their golden leaves sparkle in the sunlight. Under the lean-to, the Forest Service has provided some interpretive material about Poshuouinge.

The hike from your car to the lean-to and back is one mile and is recommended for those in good physical condition, with no health impediments. Proper footwear is a must, as the trails are not regularly cleared.

SONG OF THE SKY LOOM

O, our Mother the Earth,
O, our Father the Sky,
Your children are we, and with tired backs
we bring you the gifts that you love.

—San Ildefonso poem

ABIQUIU

Enduring Faith and an Artist's Abode

Lo que no se puede remediar, hay que aguntar.
(What cannot be remedied, must be endured.)

⊕ **Approximate Distance: 2 miles**
Approximate Time: 1 hour (2 hours with O'Keeffe studio tour)

FROM THE ABANDONED TEWA settlement of Poshuouinge, continue 2¾ miles northwestward on US 84 to the picturesque village of Abiquiu (*AH-bee-cue*, Tewa for timber point), a town steeped in unusual history. Beneath a quilt of fertile fields and majestic mesas lies Abiquiu's troubled past; a few reminders linger still.

Site 1: Old Abiquiu ⅍ *Haunting Shell of the Past*

Approximately three-quarters of a mile up the road from Poshuouinge on the right are the skeletal remains of an 18th century Spanish adobe church. It stands on the land of an abandoned settlement formally known as *Santa Rosa de Lima de Abiquiu*. Within the confines of this church, early inhabitants would take refuge from attacking nomadic Indians, a frequent occurrence.

Time and weather have had their way with the roof of the structure, but some of its walls remain steadfast. The coffin-like, rectangular, single nave design is typical of 17th and 18th century churches built in Mexico, a style roughly replicated in New Mexico. Although the community that originally surrounded this building moved to its present-day location two miles to the west, the church stands as a relic of a time long gone.

The early life and times of Abiquiu were typical of Spanish colonial settlements in New Mexico. Far from wealthier Spain and

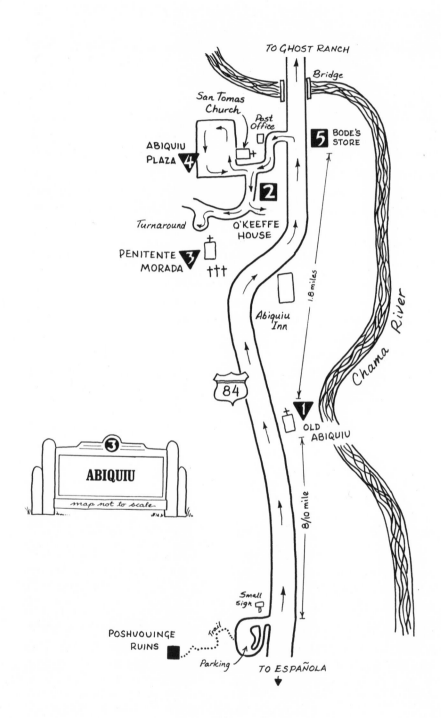

TO GHOST RANCH

Bridge

San Tomas
Church

Post
Office

ABIQUIU
PLAZA **4**

5 BODE'S
STORE

2

Turnaround

O'KEEFFE
HOUSE

PENITENTE
MORADA **3** †††

1.8 miles

Abiquiu
Inn

Chama River

84

1

OLD
ABIQUIU

8/10 mile

3

ABIQUIU

map not to scale

POSHUOUINGE
RUINS

Small
Sign

Trail

Parking

TO ESPAÑOLA

Mexico, from which supplies were meager and infrequent, local inhabitants had to develop ways to sustain themselves.

Farmers for the most part, they created *acequias* (irrigation ditches) which ensured a sharing of precious water. They fashioned tools and plows by hand from local materials, made simple furnishings for their earthen-floor homes, wove cloth and preserved produce. Poor but proud, these people survived by determination and self-reliance within a mutually-supportive community.

Old Abiquiu was constantly threatened by Ute, Navajo, Apache, and Comanche bands. Raids on Pueblo and Spanish settlements for food, horses and other livestock, and occasionally slaves, were disturbingly common. Settlers were finally forced to move to a more defensible position, on a nearby hill overlooking the Chama River.

The resettled Abiquiu, where you will arrive in a moment, was initially inhabited by *genízaros* (*hay-NEE-sah-rows*). Genízaros were Native Americans who had been kidnapped by nomadic tribes. These captives were then sold as slaves to well-to-do Spanish families at annual trade fairs held at Taos. Under their new patrons, they were baptized, given the Spanish family name and indentured as servants for a specific time period. Once free, genízaros had no homes to return to and no land or livestock. Many did what many of the dispossessed do today—join the army. Spanish governors found genízaro soldiers quite useful, stationing them along frontiers as buffers to thwart nomadic marauders.

By 1776, Padres Dominguez and Escalante were attempting to establish a route westward to California and reported visiting a sizeable community at Abiquiu. The population, composed of both Indian and Spanish residents, included 46 genízaro families.

Abiquiu's importance grew. It became a stop along the Old Spanish Trail to the Pacific Coast. By the early 1820s mountain men brought beaver and other pelts to the village, now a trading center as well as an agricultural area.

During the Mexican-American War, the U.S. Army established a military post in the village after occupying Santa Fe in August 1846 and laying claim to New Mexico. Villagers, still subject to raids by nomadic peoples, welcomed the American presence. At the same time they resisted the imposition of an Anglo culture. Hostilities between raiding Indians and Abiquiu's settlers ended in 1849 when a peace treaty was signed by the United States and the Ute Nation.

Continuing up the highway from the old church toward Abiquiu, farmland, orchards and stately old cottonwood trees come into view. Photo possibilities offer themselves in every season. Approximately two miles beyond the old church ruins, look for a sign indicating a left-hand turn into the village. Turn left, drive past the post office and continue up the hill.

At the top you may see a sign asking visitors not to take photographs in the village. Please respect this request. Just past this sign, on the left behind a large hedge, a long curving adobe wall marks the western boundary of the home of Georgia O'Keeffe.

Stop 2: O'Keeffe House

Where I was born, and where and how I lived is unimportant.
It is what I have done with where I have been that should be important.
—*O'Keeffe* (in *Georgia O'Keeffe—American and Modern*, by Charles C. Eldredge)

Georgia O'Keeffe, an icon in the annals of American Art, fell in love with the broad unobstructed views of sky, mountain, river and trees of northern New Mexico. Captivated by its beauty, she did what now a long line of Anglos have done: moved here.

The artist began life on her family's 400-acre farm November 15, 1887 near Sun Prairie, Wisconsin. She was the second of six children. In her bloodline she carried the pioneering spirit that drew her grandparents to the farmlands of the upper Midwest.

Georgia Totto O'Keeffe was named for her maternal grandfather, George Totto, a liberty-loving Hungarian count exiled after having taken part in a failed rebellion against the Austrian-Hungarian Empire. He and his family came to America and bought farmland in Wisconsin.

Georgia's paternal grandparents also left the country of their birth when their wool business in Ireland was no longer viable. Grandmother O'Keeffe, who lived next door to Georgia's childhood home, was an amateur artist with whom Georgia had a warm, loving relationship.

Growing up on a farm, the artist was exposed to the glories of nature, the birth and death of animals, and the daily struggle of rural living. She saw her father as a hero. When not working in the fields,

Francis O'Keeffe played the fiddle to entertain the family. His pockets seemed to hold an everlasting supply of gifts of sweets. That she came from people who worked with their hands was a continuing source of pride to Georgia.

While her father was engaged with the outer of world of natural things, her mother Ida dealt with the world of ideas. She read her children adventure stories and biographies, helped shape the local school's curriculum and invited schoolteachers to live in her home.

Early on, young Georgia's artistic skills became evident. The sisters at the Catholic school she attended pushed her to do her best. And she won awards.

When the farm could no longer support the family, the O'Keeffes moved to Virginia. There Francis ran a creamery and Ida a boarding house. Georgia attended the University of Virginia and was praised by her art professors. She also studied at the Chicago Art Institute, where John Vanderpoel taught her, "The purpose of art is to create beauty."

In her mid-twenties, O'Keeffe accepted a position as art teacher in Amarillo, Texas. She insisted her students draw from their imagination rather than do copy work (as she had been instructed at the Chicago Institute); the school board considered her teaching method radical.

Enrolling in a summer teachers' accreditation program at Columbia University in New York, Miss O'Keeffe also took courses at the Art Students League. There she studied with William Merritt Chase, an artist known for his impressionist, lush brush style. At Columbia she met Anna Pollitzer who introduced Georgia to Gallery 291 on Park Avenue. Its owner was the world-famous photographer Alfred Stieglitz, a man whose passion for the arts was boundless. In his gallery he exhibited avant-garde European artists, such as Picasso, Matisse and Bracque. He also featured the work of as yet unknown American artists John Marin, Charles Demuth, Arthur Dove, Marsden Hartley, and Paul Strand. By giving public lectures, Stieglitz promoted these innovative artists, presented his philosophy of art and shared his love of creativity.

After entering this new world, Georgia's life would never be the same. Stieglitz, twenty-four years her senior, was to become her teacher, publicist, agent, business manager, lover, and eventually her

husband. Their special collaborative relationship has been the subject of numerous books, as well as theater and television productions.

O'Keeffe first saw New Mexico while driving to California with her sister in 1917. She did not return until 1929 when, as a guest of art patron Mabel Dodge Luhan, she was introduced into a circle of writers, artists, photographers and poets in Taos. Describing that summer's stay, Georgia wrote to a friend, "It has been like the wind and the sun ... there doesn't seem to have been a crack of the waking day or night that wasn't full." At that time she also discovered Ghost Ranch, soon to be her summer home (see *Part Five*).

Stieglitz, who is purported to have said that the United States ended at the Mississippi River, never shared her trips to New Mexico. O'Keeffe travelled back and forth from New York until his death in 1946. Then New Mexico became her permanent home. During her summer sojourns, she came upon the village of Abiquiu, 16 miles southeast of Ghost Ranch. She persisted in a search for a winter home there. "I must have it," she said when she saw a dilapidated, three-acre compound. Owner Jose Chavez offered to sell it to her, but she thought his price too high. In 1826, a previous owner had bought the property for one cow, one calf, one bushel of corn, and a serape.

When Jose passed on, his son sold the compound to the Catholic Parish for a nominal sum. The church allowed the Abiquiu Livestock Association to house its pigs and cows there. Georgia badgered the church until they finally sold her the "hacienda" for $10 in December 1945. At about the same time, the artist had made a sizeable donation to the parish.

Five decaying buildings sat on three acres. For three years O'Keeffe and her sometime companion, Maria Chabot, oversaw major renovations to the property. It was difficult to acquire building materials in New Mexico after World War II because most were earmarked for the construction of the town of Los Alamos and a permanent research laboratory there.

Although an outsider and reclusive, Miss O'Keeffe's presence was accepted by the villagers. She influenced their lives in numerous ways:

through scholarships, employment and church donations. She was only one of two Anglos in the traditional Spanish town (the other was Martin Bode), yet she never learned to speak Spanish. Her long-time gardener spoke no English: he and O'Keeffe were often overheard in lively discussions during planting season.

The artist loved watercress salad made from greens freshly gathered from her garden and a nearby spring. She was making her own yogurt before others had learned how to spell it. A healthy lifestyle, which included long walks in the desert, and actively creative impulses surely contributed to her long life.

In the early years of her career, she used watercolors, charcoals and oils to explore the possibilities of abstract art. But when she came to the Southwest, her artistic vocabulary expanded as she focused on objects found in her new setting.

Soon the artist was creating realistic paintings of flowers, bones, churches, hills, and landscapes. She painted thick, black crosses that overwhelmed the majesty of the mountains and sky of northern New Mexico. O'Keeffe simplified the monumental forms now part of her everyday life. Examples include the 'Blue River' (Rio Chama), Pedernal, and the red and yellow cliffs of Ghost Ranch. Her canvasses make marvelous use of the "painter's palette of colors" found in New Mexico: the tender greens of spring, the delicate pinks of sunrise, the glowing purples of sunset, and the sensuous red and yellows of the cliffs surrounding Ghost Ranch.

How sad then that all these colors were denied her when she reached her mid-seventies. The artist became afflicted with a gradu-ally progressing blindness. In 1973 she hired Juan Hamilton, son of a Presbyterian minister, to help her with menial tasks. Hamilton was a college graduate and a trained sculptor. The two became close companions despite a wide disparity in their ages. Their relationship included traveling together, arranging the disposition of papers and works of Alfred Stieglitz, and exhibiting in dual shows. O'Keeffe, under Hamilton's tutelage, experimented with clay and was encour-aged to continue painting by him and other friends. Assistants were hired to help with her painting.

The artist died March 6, 1986 in Santa Fe in her 99th year. At her request, her ashes were scattered from her favorite mountain, Cerro Pedernal (see *Part Four*). In her will she left Hamilton a large number of her drawings, watercolors, pastels and paintings. He was deeded her Ghost Ranch home, as well as books, records and other personal effects. Hamilton continues to participate in the perpetuation of her artistic legacy by serving on the board of the Georgia O'Keeffe Foundation.

To reach the driveway of O'Keeffe's Abiquiu home you follow the hedge and adobe wall around the curve to the left until you see the entrance. Please do not enter the driveway unless you have arranged for a visit. Spontaneous stops aren't permitted. Tours of limited size are offered for $20 per person at this writing. For a schedule of tours, fees and other information, call the Georgia O'Keeffe Foundation at (505) 685-4539, Monday through Friday 9 a.m. to 5 p.m. Since bookings are set months in advance, be advised to call well before your planned visit.

Not able to tour the artist's home? Don't feel too disheartened—we'll share what we discovered. Miss O'Keeffe's taste in furnishings, while contemporary for its time (1950s), was austere. She insisted the house not be solely Spanish, Indian or modern, but a blending of styles. Two-foot thick adobe walls were broken through so that tiny Spanish windows could be replaced with large ones (a great advantage for those taking an "exterior tour" of the buildings). Fireplaces were built in every room. The carriage house, or storage area for wagons, was converted into O'Keeffe's large studio and an adjacent small bedroom. From her studio and bedroom not only did she receive the northern light so desired by artists, but also a spectacular view of the valley below and the mountains in the distance.

The earthen floors you'll see were common in Spanish and Indian homes. They're hard but vulnerable, hence the request that high-heeled shoes not be worn when you tour the house. The kitchen appliances (*circa* 1950) may produce a nostalgic smile for some—the Kelvinator mangel period piece is not to be missed.

The white walls of O'Keeffe's home were often bare of artworks. On occasion, she was known to hang part of her much-loved Arthur Dove collection or her own paintings—but not for long. After one or two weeks she would remove them, believing they could not be truly appreciated if they remained longer.

What was special about Georgia O'Keeffe's art? She ignored the march of "isms" that were imported from Europe. She developed her own "in-your-face" view of the world, a perception that blended both her American roots and her idiosyncratic personality. She infused an emotional intensity into the subject of her work. Her landscapes present a bold yet sensitive rendering of color and form. Her flowers have been compared to human portraits. Her animal skulls make you look in a new way at objects often ignored or thought unpleasant. Georgia O'Keeffe created an *oeuvre* so original that even she thought there was no need for her signature. When asked by a New York reporter why she rarely signed her work, she said, "Would you sign your face?" Indeed, her art is so distinctive and recognized the world over that a signature is superfluous.

In late 1995, the Museum of New Mexico announced the creation of a Georgia O'Keeffe museum in Santa Fe, causing a stir throughout the art world. There have been other attempts to create a space devoted exclusively to her work, but none proved feasible. **The Georgia O'Keeffe Museum** is today probably the only museum in the U.S. dedicated to one woman's work. Located on Johnson Street near the Plaza in downtown Santa Fe, with 10,000 square feet of exhibit space, the Georgia O'Keeffe Museum is privately endowed but is operated jointly in an arrangement with New Mexico's Museum of Fine Arts. It opened in July 1997.

Site 3: Penitente Morada ᨠ *Penance and Presence*

From the driveway of the O'Keeffe house, continue along the dirt lane for a short distance as it curves up a hill to the right. On your left is a low, windowless structure—a Penitente *morada*. It was built by the Pious Fraternity of Jesus of Nazareth, one of many confraternities commonly known as the Penitente Brotherhood. A morada functions

as an intimate sanctuary, informal court, and a place to hold vigils for the dead.

The rituals that take place within these walls are by tradition private. However, during Holy Week Penitente processions and prayers become public. In years gone by, barefoot, scantily clad, and carrying crosses, the Brothers could be seen flagellating themselves with yucca branches, as they made their way over the nearby hills.

When Spanish priests were banished from New Mexico in 1821 (after Mexico won its independence from Spain), isolated village residents turned to the Penitente Brotherhood for the maintenance of rituals and practices fundamental to the Catholic faith. The brotherhood's rise to power in the community and their use of self-flagellation as penance became grounds for rejection by the church hierarchy. As a consequence, the Penitentes built moradas, and there held rituals secretly.

It took almost a hundred years for the Penitentes to be accepted back into the folds of the Church. They then were acknowledged for their religious services to the community, which included supplying provisions for the poor and needy (such as a pile of wood left anonymously beside a widow's door).

The Abiquiu morada is reputed to be the oldest in New Mexico. Over a period of 200 years, many moradas have been neglected or abandoned, burned, and sometimes vandalized. In September 1992 this morada was vandalized. It was rebuilt and rededicated the following April. Please observe the No Trespassing sign while appreciating from the road this historic structure and the crosses so essential to the Penitente faith.

Dios tarda pero no olvida.
(God may be late but He doesn't forget.)

Site 4: Plaza and Church 〰 *Sustenance and Spirit*

Retrace the route down the hill past the O'Keeffe house. Before descending back to the highway, turn left at the end of the O'Keeffe property. Take note of the abandoned adobe building on the left. Although its mud bricks are disintegrating, the traditional dirt roof still supports native grasses and a *cholla cactus.*

You may have noticed this prevalent cactus in your travels in northern New Mexico. In early June it has striking magenta flowers, which are followed by yellow fruits that often last until the next blooming season. For centuries cholla has been an important edible. And for good reason: two tablespoons of cooked cholla buds have as much calcium as a glass of milk.

Go past the abandoned building and drive onto the village plaza. This open area, the heart of the town where people socialized, traded and worshipped, retains the flavor of Spanish settlements in the New World. The most striking architectural feature is the large **Church of San Tomas** on the right. Beautiful wood carving adorns the building, characteristic of churches built during the Spanish colonial period (1698–1821). The door is normally locked except during services. For a look at the interior, inquire at the building to the right of the church. A courtesy donation to the parish will be appreciated.

A small store, a parish building and several private homes complete the plaza. Taking a stroll about the village will enable you to experience the feeling of being in Spanish Colonial New Mexico. When you're ready to leave, return past the old adobe building and make your descent to the highway. Our tour continues to the left, but we strongly recommend a stop at **Bode's General Store**, directly across the highway.

Stop 5: Bode's Store ❧
Horse collars, Liniments, and Lamp Wicks

Beyond its slamming screen door, in a large sun-filled space, hundreds of "things of yesteryear" and "things of today" nudge each other on neatly-stacked shelves. In addition to snacks, sundries and suntan lotions, this old-fashioned grocery and hardware store has food in freezers, canned and boxed goods, the latest in fishing gear, plumbing supplies, boots, hats, and building materials. Situated in this agricultural valley, Bode's also stocks animal feed, farmers' seed, local produce and crafts, and sometimes still-warm horno-baked bread and hot tamales sold at the cash register. Need rustic porcelain kitchen utensils, a horse collar, oil lamp wicks, a corn cob bread mold, or a chimney for your wood stove? This is the place!

Customers in and around Abiquiu have been shopping at Bode's since 1919. Some still recall their neighbor, a dark-clad artist from the east, walking up and down its aisles. Early on, Martin Bode, a German immigrant, established the still-living tradition of carrying items not easily obtained elsewhere in New Mexico.

Maintaining this business practice, Dennis Liddy, who bought Bode's in 1994, still features McLean's Volcanic Water Liniment (said to cure all aches and pains), small wood-framed tin laundry washboards, and a mustard plaster (helped by an image of Our Lady of Guadalupe) to combat chest congestion. So now's the time to stock up on things ordinary and extraordinary! While shopping, don't miss the enormous mounted elk head with its huge rack of antlers, purportedly felled by bow and arrow by a local resident. Before you depart, check your restroom needs and your fuel gauge.

"If you ever go to New Mexico,
it will itch you for the rest of your life."

—*Georgia O'Keeffe*

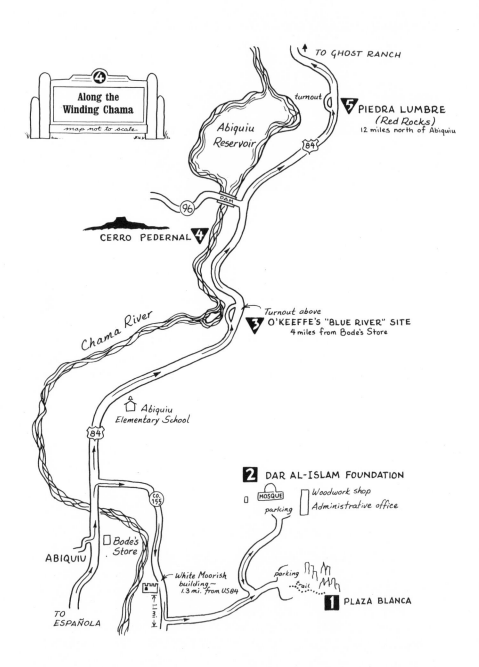

④

Along the Winding Chama

map not to scale

TO GHOST RANCH

turnout

5 PIEDRA LUMBRE
(Red Rocks)
12 miles north of Abiquiu

Abiquiu Reservoir

84

96 DAM

CERRO PEDERNAL **4**

Chama River

Turnout above

3 O'KEEFFE'S "BLUE RIVER" SITE
4 miles from Bode's Store

Abiquiu Elementary School

84

2 DAR AL-ISLAM FOUNDATION

MOSQUE   Woodwork shop
parking   Administrative office

CO. 155

Bode's Store

ABIQUIU

White Moorish building—
1.3 mi. from US 84

parking

trail

1 PLAZA BLANCA

TO ESPAÑOLA

Part Four

ALONG THE WINDING CHAMA

Sand Castles, Dome of Islam, Fire Rocks

¿Quién sabe en qué palo iré en parar la paloma?
(Who knows on which branch the dove will land?)

⊛ **Approximate Distance: 18 miles**
Approximate Time: 1¾ hours (with 20 minutes at Plaza Blanca)

ON THIS PART OF YOUR JOURNEY, Mother Nature may amaze you with her child-like treatment of the gray sediment at Plaza Blanca, her sense of humor at Cerro Pedernal, and her artistic sensibility at the red rocks. You may also have an unexpected spiritual experience. And you can walk where Georgia O'Keeffe walked—which some might consider a spiritual experience, too!

Turn right from Bode's parking lot and drive 7/10 mile northeast on US 84. Turn right again, onto a small dirt road marked by a blue and yellow road marker reading, Rio Arriba County 155. Down this road about three miles are Plaza Blanca (the white place) and the Dar al-Islam Mosque.

Stop 1: Plaza Blanca ❧ *Weathered Works*

The route to Plaza Blanca necessitates crossing an arroyo which lies about 100 feet from the highway turnoff. Arroyos, generally dry streambeds, are occasionally flooded by cloudbursts. If there is water or mud in the arroyo in front of you, don't cross it. If the way is clear, and it generally is, follow the road as it bears to the right. Here the cottonwood trees are up close and personal. Note how these trees trace the path of the Chama River. Commonly found near water, they and their close cousin the aspen make excellent drum material. Archaic people, as well more modern Indians, have been know to

75

extract liquid from cottonwood leaves by boiling them, and then using this juice for the relief of pain.

After driving 1.3 miles, a small white building with unusual Islamic-like architecture appears on the right. Less than a mile further, you come upon a midwestern farmhouse (what next!). Continue on for about one-half mile and you will see a sign on the right directing you to turn left toward the Dar al-Islam Mosque. After half a mile on this private dirt lane, you face a fork in the road. Take the right fork for a tenth of a mile, and you will arrive at a small parking area. Before you is a startling natural wonder—Plaza Blanca.

Appearing like sand castles frozen in time, **Plaza Blanca** is the residue of earth-shaking activity—the same eruptions that caused the Jemez Mountains that have been on your left as you traveled northwest. Geologists say violent earth movements and volcanoes occurred in this area sometime between one and ten million years ago.

Georgia O'Keeffe came to paint here, and named this spot "The White Place." The artist is said to have been fascinated by these formations of ash, mud and sediment. The property is currently owned by the Dar al-Islam Foundation which graciously allows public access.

You may never have walked in a place such as this, so lace on your Reeboks—and don't forget your camera, for there are excellent photo opportunities here. One such is the solitary tamarisk tree (salt cedar) standing at the base of the sand castles. In the fall this slender tree with feathery leaves dons a glowing orange foliage. Non-native to New Mexico, in some areas tamarisk is crowding out native willows along New Mexico's waterways.

Return to the fork in the road and proceed on the other fork slowly up the hill. The surface of the lane has deteriorated and may be rutted from recent rains. The mosque is only half a mile further on.

Stop 2: Dar al-Islam Mosque

Middle East Meets the Southwest

While northern New Mexico is predominantly Catholic, people of diverse religions and on various spiritual paths have been attracted to and accepted in the region. Muslims making a place for themselves in the desert may not be unusual, but finding an adobe-domed mosque in sight of Georgia O'Keeffe's home in Hispanic Abiquiu gives one pause.

The Dar al-Islam (an Islamic name meaning "place of surrender") Foundation was formed in 1979 by Nurideen Durkee of the famous Durkee Spice family, who was instrumental in purchasing 1000 acres here for $1,372,000. Durkee said the organization was established "to radiate a living example of Islam and Islamic life and education." The foundation is based in Abiquiu with an office in Washington, D.C.

The architectural gem on the property is the mosque, or *masjid*, and its adjoining buildings. In 1980 Hassan Fathy came to Abiquiu to create the facility. An Egyptian architect and author, Fathy is celebrated in the Islamic world for his revival of the use of domes, vaults and arches in Islamic structures. In this mosque, Fathy employed architectural techniques used 5,000 years ago in Egypt's Valley of the Kings. Adobe bricks (mud mixed with straw and dried in the sun) were the primary material used in its construction, and were laid up mostly by the hands of a host of community supporters. The mosque

represents not only a symbol of religious faith, but Hassan Fathy's philosophy, "One man alone cannot build a house, but ten men can build ten houses."

Facing east toward Mecca, the mosque provides space for daily Islamic practices. Within the structure, open 24 hours each day, you will find a tiled area to wash your feet before praying and a separate area for women. The interior walls are plastered with white gypsum, and the floors are covered with traditional *hasira* (prayer mats made of straw).

In the 1990s adjacent to the mosque, a *madressah*, or study facility with dormitory quarters, was completed. Dar al-Islam holds an annual conference for social studies teachers interested in learning about Islam, and also offers an intensive study program for students of Islam. These projects are designed as part of the organization's mission: to inform the public about the meaning of their faith.

Beginning in 1993, Dar al-Islam in Abiquiu has been the site of a powwow for groups of Muslims from around the country. Borrowing from the Native American concept of a gathering of peoples, this event brings together different Islamic groups for an interchange of ideas and beliefs.

Behind the mosque are the administrative offices. Attached is the **Andaluz Woodwork** operation. It is run by one of the Islamic families presently living in the area who are associated with Dar al-Islam.

Visitors are welcome at all times and photographs are permitted. Weekdays you can check with the administrative office for additional information. The study and dormitory facilities are available for rent to groups, (505) 685-4515. There are public restrooms here, but they don't have running water.

Before leaving, don't miss the glorious view of the Chama River Valley and Abiquiu below. Return to your car and retrace your route back to the fork, to County Road 155, and US 84, 3.5 miles away.

Site 3: The Chama River ᨠ *Georgia Loved It*

Make a right-hand turn onto US 84. To arrive at Site 3 (and a lovely place for photographs) you need to drive ahead about four miles. Along the way, you'll see Abiquiu Elementary School on your right. Behind the school, an extension of the same ash and silt formations of Plaza Blanca appears amongst the hills. On your left you pass farm fields, which are an eye-catching alfalfa green in the summer, thanks to irrigation from the Chama River. In these fields cattle grazing on the pastoral bottomlands are a familiar sight.

A little further on you will spot the "house of many styles" down on the left. This small abode is round like a Navajo hogan, has protruding vigas as in Santa Fe Pueblo style homes, and its roof, instead of being completely flat, is bordered by a curvilinear design. New Mexico is a land of many owner-built experiments in architecture!

As the road begins to climb, the rock columns towering on your right (reminiscent of those in Utah's Bryce Canyon) take on a reddish hue. Just before the road curves to the left, exactly four miles from County Road 155, a small turn-off appears on your left. From this site, the Chama River and the mountains above it cry out for your attention. "Ahhh!" has been spoken here more than once.

Here the Chama River emerges from a multi-colored canyon in a sweeping S-curve as it enters the valley. Immediately below, the river flows around an island, creating a pastoral scene that many have been moved to try to capture on film or sketch pad.

The source of the Chama is a section of the Rocky Mountains 75 miles to the north, just across the Colorado border. It lends its name to a New Mexico town known for hunting and fishing, about 57 miles up the road. A segment of the river draws rafters from northern New Mexico for both day and overnight trips. River-rafting on the Chama and Rio Grande can be an exciting experience in northern New Mexico. For information, call **Southwest Wilderness Adventures,** (505) 983-7262 or **Far Flung Adventures,** (505) 758-2528.

Georgia O'Keeffe painted this meandering river over and over in her "Blue River" series. Originally depicted in a realistic manner in the 1930s, the river becomes a blue abstraction in a field of green in her 1960s version. Although Miss O'Keeffe called the Chama the blue river, its Tewa name actually means red river, because it is often muddy with red earth. Two paintings of this scene by the artist are in the collection at the New Mexico Museum of Fine Art in Santa Fe.

Site 4: Cerro Pedernal 🐾 *"Where's My Head?"*

Continue climbing up the highway. When you are on the plateau above the incline, look to your left at the uniquely-shaped mountain

that stands out in the distance. This prominent 9,000-foot peak, part of the Jemez Range, appears to have lost its top. Rather than having a pointed or rounded cap like mountains nearby, its summit seems to have been sheared off by some force of nature. **Cerro Pedernal** ("flint hill" in Spanish) was important to local Indians because flint for arrowheads was found on its flanks.

Does Pedernal look familiar to you? Georgia O'Keeffe was captivated by it and included the peak in many of her landscapes. "God told me if I painted it enough I could have it," she once said.

As you continue to drive along the plateau, you will soon come to a sign for **Abiquiu Dam**, one mile ahead. You're about to enjoy another of New Mexico's visual enchantments! When you reach the turnoff for Abiquiu Dam at NM 96, an extraordinary vista opens before you. The breathtaking beauty of the next five miles on NM 84 are worthy of a trip in themselves. Before you is an open plain, partially filled with something surprising in New Mexico: a large lake created by the nearby dam. Swimming and boating opportunities are available at this recreation area run by the Bureau of Land Management. For northern New Mexicans, this is one of few fresh water lakes in the area, and many come here to enjoy summer activities.

Surrounding the lake, for as far as the eye can see, are massive cliffs layered with ribbons of color—yellows, reds, pinks and browns. What you are looking at are a series of sandstone deposits made over a 200 million-year period. These sandstones layers are capped in places with gypsum, a grayish-white mineral.

New Mexico's landscape today is dramatically different from its multiple appearances over the past 200 million years. Early on, dinosaurs roamed here. They walked on tropical floodplains covered with rivers that inundated the state. Sediment deposited by these rivers and exploding volcanoes created the lower portions of the cliffs you see.

When a more desert-like climate developed, the dinosaurs moved to the edges of rivers and marshes. Sandstones which developed during this later period now appear on the upper portion of the cliffs that surround you. Approximately 65 million years ago dinosaurs became extinct as the result of some catastrophic event. Fossils remains of these creatures can still be found in the rocks of this region.

Site 5: Piedra Lumbre ❧ *Rocks of Fire*

As you follow the route north for about four miles, the red rocks loom closer and closer. Soon you will descend down into the fiery rocks themselves. Their reddish color is due to iron oxide present in the sandstone. One of the largest of the Spanish land grants, *Piedra Lumbre* (fire rock), was named after this spot.

Turning to your left you'll find a picnic table and a magnificent view. Look up the canyon walls at the varied shapes and subtle changes in colors. A striking green band of olivine runs horizontally through the last segment of the red rocks.

Heading up the highway you will soon arrive at the legendary Ghost Ranch and its "dinosaur cemetery."

La tierra es benedición de Dios.
(The land is a blessing from God.)
—*Aurelita Eturriaga Salazar, Los Ojos*

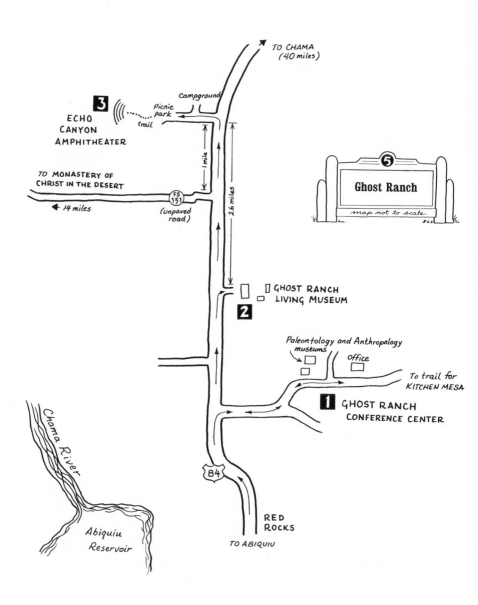

TO CHAMA
(40 miles)

Campground

3 Picnic park

ECHO
CANYON
AMPHITHEATER

trail

TO MONASTERY OF
CHRIST IN THE DESERT

1 mile

2.6 miles

FS
151

← 14 miles

(unpaved road)

⑤

Ghost Ranch

map not to scale

▯ GHOST RANCH
▫ LIVING MUSEUM

2

Paleontology and Anthropology
museums

Office

To trail for
KITCHEN MESA

1 GHOST RANCH
CONFERENCE CENTER

Chama River

84

RED
ROCKS

Abiquiu
Reservoir

TO ABIQUIU

Part Five ———————————————————————

GHOST RANCH

Bones of Dinosaurs, Tableaus of Time

Ama a tu vecino y te amará.
(Love your neighbor and he will love you.)

⊙ **Approximate Time: 2 hours (without side trip to monastery)**
Approximate Distance: 6 miles

FOR ONE HUNDRED MILLION YEARS, strange four-limbed reptiles, some almost 75 feet long and weighing 10 tons, roamed this land. Mysteries about these reptiles, called dinosaurs, have long piqued the imagination of both children and adults. How did they evolve? Why did they all die so suddenly 65 million years ago? And would we be here if they hadn't perished? Answers to these mysteries are slowing surfacing as paleontologists unearth dinosaurs bones in different places around the world. One such place in northern New Mexico is at Ghost Ranch.

Stop 1: Ghost Ranch ಇ *Dinosaur Boneyard*

This 21,000-acre ranch was won by a cowboy during a poker game. Dick Plaff, the lucky cowboy, then sold his winnings to Phoebe and Arthur Pack in 1933. The Packs created a resort for wealthy vacationers, a working dude ranch and guest house set amidst coral-colored rocks, wild burros, *cholla* cactus, and an occasional rattlesnake.

Many stories are told about how Ghost Ranch got its unusual name. Before the Packs arrived, Spanish natives in the area referred to it as *El Rancho de los Brujos* (the Ranch of the Witches). They claimed a red-haired demon roamed the land; others said a winged cow flew over at dusk; still others believed a 360-foot snake called *Vivaron* slithered across the property. More current is the story of a murderous husband who slew his brother, having caught him in an adulterous affair with his wife. People say they hear the brother's cries echoing off the canyon walls.

Ghost Ranch was once part of a 1776 land grant given by the Spanish king to Pedro Martin Serrano. Through the years, it has been divided by heirs and sold off in small parcels.

After owning the ranch for twenty-two years, the Packs donated the land and its buildings to the Presbyterian Church in 1955. The church uses Ghost Ranch as a national adult study center. Ghost Ranch offers seminars in archaeology, paleontology, theology, education, and language, as well as numerous other topics. These courses are open to the public regardless of religious affiliation. Popular Elderhostel programs are available in the spring and fall. Rooms and camping facilities are rented to passing travelers when not filled by seminar participants.

As a steward of the northern New Mexico's environment, Ghost Ranch management has pioneered the use of low-cost solar energy and established a research farm. Because this dry highland area receives an average annual rainfall of only 10 inches, pastureland is at a premium. Ghost Ranch, in a good-neighbor policy, allows its irrigated and vast acreage to be used as a community resource. From December through April, local ranchers, owners of small herds, graze their stock on ranch land at less than standard grazing fees.

Where cattle graze now, dinosaurs once walked. In 1947 the bones of *Coelophysis,* one of the earliest dinosaurs ever found in North America, were discovered on this ranch. Hundreds of complete Coelophysis skeletons were found here in a once-marshy grave. About 200 million years ago, when the land was less arid, a flood deposited these remains in a mass burial. This remarkable finding led to Ghost Ranch's designation as a Registered National Landmark. Research relating to dinosaurs followed, resulting in the establishment of the **Ruth Hall Museum of Paleontology**. Though small, this museum makes a large impression on all its visitors.

Adjoining this facility is another museum devoted to anthropology, which includes artifacts and information on Native American people who lived in the area as long ago as 10,000 B.C. Both museums are open from 9 a.m. to noon Tuesday through Saturday, and 1 to 5 p.m. Tuesday through Sunday. Both are closed Mondays. For a special summer treat, search among the eaves of the museum

courtyard and its outside walls for mud nests. If your timing is right, mother barn swallows may be feeding a chorus of chicks lining the edges of the nests.

While on a visit to New Mexico in 1934, Georgia O'Keeffe stumbled upon Ghost Ranch and took a room for the night. Fascinated by the landscape, she stayed the entire summer. This began her pattern of summer retreats to this beautiful valley. In the sixth summer she returned to find the house she had always rented occupied by someone else. Infuriated, Georgia insisted the Packs sell her the property. They did.

After the rest of the ranch was donated to the Presbyterian Church, Georgia kept her cottage. Always shown respect for her privacy, she quickly found the Presbyterians to be good neighbors. When fire destroyed their headquarters building in 1983, O'Keeffe gave $50,000 toward its reconstruction. Her Ghost Ranch home, not easily visible, is not open to the public.

In her book *Portrait of an Artist: A Biography of Georgia O'Keeffe*, Laurie Lisle says the setting of the artist's Ghost Ranch home was the inspiration for the red and yellow cliffs, bones, blossoms, desert skies, and clouds depicted in so many of O'Keeffe's paintings.

Visiting Ghost Ranch in spring and summer is especially lovely if there has been sufficient rain. Barn swallows swoop, and the air is permeated with the smell of sagebrush. Wildflowers, such as *red paintbrush, magenta bee-balm* (mountain oregano), the white trumpet-like flowers of the *jimsonweed* (one of O'Keeffe's favorites), yellow clusters of *yarrow*, and the pink puffs of *Apache plume* pepper the landscape. Varieties of wild plants in the northern New Mexico region exceed well over a thousand, but they are not usually abundant, and so you may have to search around to see them or take one of the suggested hikes.

Should you wish to linger longer—take a course, spend a week— call (505) 685-4333 or write to Ghost Ranch, Abiquiu, New Mexico 87510. When on site, you can stop at the office for more information and buy sundries and snacks at the attached gift shop (open afternoons with hours varying by season and seminar times). There are three wonderful hiking trails here (see *Hiking* appendix).

Stop 2: Ghost Ranch Living Museum *Fur and Feathers*

Upon leaving Ghost Ranch, turn right on US 84 and proceed 1.7 miles to the **Ghost Ranch Living Museum.** Don't let the name confuse you; the Living Museum is run by the Carson National Forest, not the Presbyterians. Its history, however, is intertwined with its neighbor, Ghost Ranch.

This museum was the brainchild of Arthur Pack, developer of Ghost Ranch, who provided funds for the project. It was inspired by the Arizona-Sonora Desert Museum near Tucson, which Pack also helped found. At the time Pack gave Ghost Ranch to the Presbyterians, he wanted to give the Living Museum to Carson National Forest. An unusual swap occurred.

The Ghost Ranch Conference Center gave the Ghost Ranch Living Museum to the Carson National Forest in exchange for land which was under the management of the Forest Service. However, the question of ownership of this land was disputed by local Hispanic families. For generations, these people felt entitled to use the land as part of land grants given them by the Spanish king. This long-time use was honored when the Presbyterians gave the land back to the Hispanic claimants. Disputes between entitlement through Spanish land grants and the jurisdiction of the United States federal government over public lands continue to this day throughout northern New Mexico.

Here at Ghost Ranch Living Museum, injured and orphaned animals native to nearby forests and desert-like land have found a loving home. Entering the building, you first encounter an exhibit room of changing displays. On a 1996 visit, this room featured an exhibit on sustaining aspen ecosystems which included live trees.

Take a walk along the short loop path behind the main building where you'll meet the orphaned and injured animals and birds. Unable to live on their own in the wild, these creatures find sanctuary here. As you stroll, you pass native trees and plants with interpretive signs. We recently saw golden and bald eagles, red-tailed and Swainson's hawks, great horned owls, coyote, elk, cougar, muledeer bucks, a mountain lion named Harriet, and a roly-poly black bear called Horendo. Horendo was found wailing his heart out beside his dead mother along a highway north of Ghost Ranch.

The **Beaver Museum** includes extensive information on these industrious creatures, an exhibit on minerals, and a reptile wing where you can see a large Western diamond-backed rattlesnake, indigenous to the area. Just outside, Wally the Beaver (Remember *Leave It to Beaver?*) may come right up to the fence to say hello.

The Living Museum has an observation tower that provides excellent views of the spectacular colored cliffs embracing the area. If you'd like to learn the geological names of the fabulous rocks, go to the right of Harriet the mountain lion's home. There you'll see a series of telescopes, accompanied by descriptions, to let you look at individual formations off in the distance.

A recently-erected building contains "Gateway to the Past," an exhibit about New Mexico history, culture and heritage. If you visited Poshuouinge, you might enjoy the aerial photograph of those ruins, as well as the photographs of the Chama Valley shown here.

Outside the museum, the U.S. Soil Conservation Service has set up a range management demonstration area to assist local ranchers. The condition of rangeland has declined dramatically over the years since livestock was first introduced to the region. A model ranch in the display emphasizes basic management principles. The Soil Conservation Service believes that if the techniques suggested are followed the land can be restored close to its original condition.

Ghost Ranch Living Museum is open 8 a.m. to 4 p.m. daily except Mondays and major holidays. A gift shop is open from 10 a.m. to 3 p.m. from March through October. The Forest Service requests a donation of $3 per adult and $2 per child.

Stop 3: Echo Canyon Amphitheater ❧ *Desert Delights*

After traveling 2.6 miles north on US 84 you arrive at the apex of your journey, **Echo Canyon Amphitheater**. This is a fine place for a picnic if you have not had lunch. Drive a quarter mile down the road to the left off US 84 and you'll find a picnic ground with shaded tables and nearby portable toilets. To the right is a campground. Both are maintained by the Carson National Forest.

Echo Canyon is named for the natural rock amphitheater that towers in front of you. It can be reached by taking the easy, ten-minute "Trail to the Echo" leading from the picnic area. At the end of the trail you come to the echo chamber. Call into the rock cliffs and your voice comes right back to you. Children love to hear their voices echo and to have clear, loud conversations with each other. Mother Nature created this phenomenal concave formation through the slow and gentle touch of wind and rain. A surprise at the echo site are five Douglas firs. To find these trees—the largest native species in New Mexico—at under 7000 feet altitude is very unusual.

You pass through 100 million years of geologic history as you walk to the amphitheater. The rocks towering above you are layered in distinct strata, each representing a specific period when sediment was deposited. The white rock on the top is composed of limestone, shale and gypsum; named the *Toldito Formation*, it was deposited 100 million years ago on the bottom of a shallow lake.

Below the Toldito are the beige and yellow sandstones of the *Entrada Formation*. Winds deposited sand dunes here 150 million years ago, which over time became sandstone. An interesting characteristic of the Entrada is that it erodes into concave amphitheaters, such as the one here.

At the bottom of these two formations lies the *Chinle Formation*. The soil you are standing on is crumbled Chinle sandstone, siltstone and shale. Petrified wood found in this striking reddish-hued strata indicates a dense forest once existed on this site some 200 million years ago. The Chinle Formation is also where paleontologists are finding Coelophysis and other dinosaur fossils.

In the summertime, you can hear the high-pitched calls of *white-throated swifts*. When you look up, you'll spot small, dark shapes flitting about. These birds nest in the cavities of the cliffs. They are black and white underneath and spend much of their day aloft hunting insects. Swifts are fast-flying birds with long, narrow, stiff wings and forked tails. They head south in fall to winter in southern New Mexico and Mexico. You are also apt to see and hear ravens in this area, as well as iridescent violet-green swallows. Less common, but occasionally present, are hawks and eagles of the varieties you saw at the Ghost Ranch Living Museum.

When your visit here is done, get back on US 84 for the return to Santa Fe. If you have time to explore further, a fascinating side trip awaits at a turnoff on the right, one mile down the highway. This turnoff onto National Forest Service Road 151 leads to a Benedictine monastery in the wilderness. If you would enjoy camping along the Chama River, the National Forest Service has provided primitive campsites a short distance off the road leading to the monastery.

Side trip: Monastery of Christ in the Desert

The 13-mile ride to the cloister is no quick and easy matter. It can take up to an hour, depending on road conditions. The road is most securely traversed in a four-wheel drive vehicle, for there may be ruts that a standard car can't clear without bottoming out. However, the National Forest Service grades the road now and then, making it possible for any car to make the trip most of the time. If it is raining or about to rain, however, do not attempt it.

The character of the terrain is perhaps a metaphor for the pursuit of the contemplative life that takes place at the end of the road. Key to the hardships experienced by New Mexico's early settlers was its isolation; yet isolation for the Benedictine brothers at the monastery is crucial to their search for communion with God.

While night still hovers overhead, a small group of black-cowled monks wend their way to a 4 a.m. prayer service called vigils, held in a simple but inspiring adobe sanctuary. It is one of seven periods during the day dedicated to devotional recitations. When not occupied in common prayer and ritual devotion, about twenty-five brothers raise their own food, practice choral singing, and make candles, carvings, weavings and greeting cards—and Internet websites!

Under the ancient Rule of St. Benedict, the monks consider it a duty and an honor to meet and greet visitors, including those who come to stay in their guest house. People come to Christ in the Desert from all over the world for private retreats. Guests remain for short periods in nine modest cell-like rooms. Limited space makes pre-arrangements necessary.

"We are a family," says Abbot Philip. "To the extent we can live together and solve problems is a way of measuring our closeness to God. Much time is spent in silence so that we may hear God's voice."

Vows of obedience and to a life dedicated to Christ are required for those entering the Benedictine Order. Candidates must serve a six-month period as postulant and one year as a novitiate. Once the final decision to become a Benedictine monk is made, the commitment is usually for life.

Daily life here is one of gentle routine, regulated in an atmosphere of quietude. The sparse and simple furnishings of the monastery are in marked contrast to the vivid beauty of its Chama River Canyon surroundings. The red and yellow cliffs, made familiar from Georgia O'Keeffe's work, soar majestically above, while the Chama River rushes southward, continually at work carving its path through the broad canyon.

In the works are a new cloister (sleeping quarters for the growing community of brothers), an expanded refectory (dining hall), and eventually more guest accommodations. The monastery welcomes people of all faiths, men and women (but no pets or children), for stays of a few days.

Centuries ago dedicated monks, laboring in the scriptorium of their European cloister, crafted beautifully illuminated pages of the holy scriptures. This tradition continues today at Christ in the Desert, but instead of ink and vellum, these monks use computer skills to create breathtaking Internet pages—including one for the Vatican!

While it may be physically difficult at times to reach the Monastery of Christ in the Desert, the monks can be contacted instantaneously through cyberspace: the brothers' own home page is at *http:// www.christdesert.org/pax.html*. There you will find a wealth of information about their monastic life, the Benedictine tradition, and visits to Christ in the Desert, all beautifully illuminated, of course. To make reservations to stay overnight, write to the Guestmaster at Monastery of Christ in the Desert, P.O. Box 270, Abiquiu, NM 87510, or e-mail broandre@aol.com.

> *"A Monk is a man separated from All,*
> *but is in harmony with All."*
>
> *—A Benedictine saying*

RETURN POSSIBILITIES

Lowriders, Sikh Turbans, Beauty in Bronze

⚙ **Approximate Time: 1½ hours (without meal stop)**
Approximate Distance: 67 miles

YOU ARE NOW ON YOUR WAY back to Santa Fe, yet several places of interest remain along the route. If you're still feeling adventuresome, your return trip to New Mexico's capital city presents further opportunities for exploration.

Retrace your path back along US 84 for approximately 30 miles into Española. (Now may be a good time to refer to the short stories in the appendix if you have young children on board.) It's probably late in the afternoon, and so you'll have a chance to savor the glorious light that plays over the northern New Mexico landscape at this time nearly every day.

Just a few miles north of Española, near San Juan Pueblo off US 285 is the site of **San Gabriel**, the first Spanish settlement and first capital of New Mexico (1598). Spanish culture has been dominant in this region for centuries. Treasured traditions, passed on from the *abuelos* (elders) of one generation to the next, have deeply enriched the area.

Site 1: Española ❧ *Land of the Lowrider*

When you reach the traffic light and the Conoco Station, now on your right, you are on the outskirts of Española. This town of about 15,000 is the economic center of both the Española and the Chama River valleys.

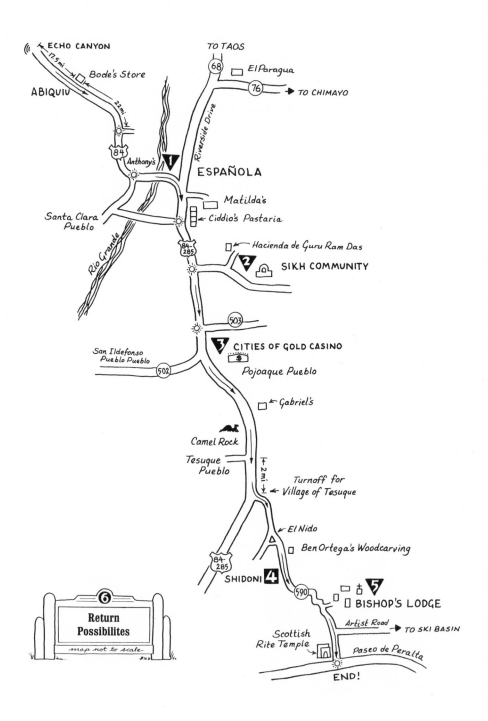

ECHO CANYON

17.5 mi

Bode's Store

ABIQUIU

22 mi

TO TAOS

68

El Paragua

76 → TO CHIMAYO

Riverside Drive

84

Anthony's

▼1

ESPAÑOLA

Matilda's

Ciddio's Pastaria

Santa Clara
Pueblo

84-285

Hacienda de Guru Ram Das

▼2

SIKH COMMUNITY

Rio Grande

503

▼3 CITIES OF GOLD CASINO

San Ildefonso
Pueblo Pueblo

502

$

Pojoaque Pueblo

Gabriel's

Camel Rock

Tesuque
Pueblo

2 mi

Turnoff for
← Village of Tesuque

← El Nido

Ben Ortega's Woodcarving

84-285

SHIDONI ■4

590

▼5

BISHOP'S LODGE

6

**Return
Possibilites**

map not to scale

Scottish
Rite Temple

Artist Road → TO SKI BASIN

Paseo de Peralta

END!

Española has been a marketplace and a gathering place since its founding in 1830. Today, the sound of creaking horse-drawn farm wagons has been replaced by the booming car stereos of modern-day romeos (and a few juliettes) who cruise the streets of this Hispanic town in their mean and clean low-riding machines.

As it may be approaching dinner time, we'd like to suggest a stop at one of several colorful restaurants. In these establishments you'll get authentic New Mexican food—and you will likely find yourself eating alongside the local crowd. Prices here are more digestible than in many Santa Fe restaurants. On your left about one and one half miles after the Conoco traffic light is **Anthony's at the Delta**, offering fine dining in a refined Southwestern setting.

Continuing southeast through town, drive past the two traffic lights just after Anthony's, following the curve to the left around the car dealership. Then you'll cross a bridge over the Rio Grande. Soon you will reach the main drag of Española; a large sign advertising tax-free cigarettes appears on your left. This shop sits on a small parcel of land owned by Santa Clara Pueblo. Here it is possible to purchase cigarettes without paying federal or state tax, a tangible expression of Native American sovereignty. Follow the sign to Santa Fe, which leads you to the right onto southbound US 84/285—called Riverside Drive in Española.

Immediately on your left look for the signs of two other eateries you might enjoy. **Ciddio's Pastaria Restaurant** is in the strip mall on the left side of Riverside Drive before the traffic light up ahead. Here you will find excellent Italian food enhanced by the flavors of northern New Mexico. The prices are reasonable and Ciddio is an amiable host.

Matilda's Cafe is just behind Ciddio's and the strip mall, on Corlett Road. Some Santa Feans say the green chile here is the best in the area. The taste of *roasted* chile in the dishes lingers on your palate, something not usually found elsewhere. Matilda has been dishing out her homemade chile for almost a quarter of a century, and she'll be happy to personally serve you, too. Unfortunately Matilda's is open only from 9 a.m. to 9 p.m. every day except Mondays. (See *Recommended Restaurants* appendix for other choices.)

"Low and Slow, Mean and Clean"

While dining, if you are seated by a window, keep an eye out for a flashy lowrider cruising Riverside Drive. Española is *the* place to

survey roads and parking lots for these unique cars. Lowriders are modified older American-made autos (1940s through 1970s) whose suspensions have been lowered so that their tailpipes nearly scrape the pavement—thus they ride *low*.

These customized vehicles, owned by young and not-so-young men and families, often pack hydraulic lifts to let the driver raise the front or rear end in characteristic lowrider fashion. Other features include special small wheels, elaborate paint jobs with airbrush murals of religious or traditional Hispanic themes, gold-plated fixtures, plush interiors and "suicide" (reverse hinged) doors. Some lowriders have embellishments totalling up to $60,000.

On weekend nights, the speed limit in Española is reputed to be five miles an hour as proud owners slowly motor along the strip, sound systems blasting, hoping to attract the opposite sex. If you want to dig deeper into this distinctive Hispanic subculture, stop at a magazine shop where you can pick up one of several national publications devoted to these cool and wild machines.

Head south on US 84/285 departing Española. As you approach the traffic light at the top of hill, just outside town, a left turn will lead you to another religious community. Here you will find people practicing an East Indian religion with an American twist in a western Indian land.

Site 2: Sikh Community ☙ *Turbans in New Mexico*

On your way to this community, behind a small hill one quarter mile off US 84/285, you will see an area covered with huge stripped ponderosa pine logs. Here *vigas* (roof beams) are being prepared. These round beams, exposed across the ceilings in the adobe-style homes of New Mexico, support traditional flat roofs. Continue for 1/10 mile and take the road to the right that cuts through a hill. Once through the hill, you'll see the golden dome of the Sikh community's temple.

The center of the largest group of Sikhs in the United States is located here. Sikhs are members of a religion founded in northern India in the 15th century. Sikhism is based on a belief in one God and a rejection of the caste system. The faith is a blend of reformed Hindu and Islamic practices—a reaction to conflicts that developed between these two major religions. In India today there are about 10 million Sikhs.

Sikh Dharma International was founded by Yogi Bhajan, an East Indian spiritual leader. The educational arm of the group is better-known as the "3HO" (Healthy, Happy, Holy Organization). Sikh Dharma International sponsors more than 100 centers in large cities and college towns around the country. Española became 3HO headquarters in 1976.

The 3HO Sikhs believe in cleanliness, cultivating spiritual and physical health, vegetarianism (differing in this regard from India's Sikhs) and a drug-free lifestyle. The community also embraces Tantrism and Kundalini Yoga. Dressed in their white garments, Sikhs in Santa Fe are a familiar sight.

Mostly American by birth, these Sikhs traditionally don't cut their hair, which is wrapped in a turban when they're in public. The turban applies pressure to the soft cranial tissue, which Sikhs believe helps balance the body and aids in mental and physical well-being. The 3HO philosophy emphasizes total involvement in local communities, with members running retail businesses and serving in municipal and state governments.

Should you like to visit their temple, drive past it and park in an area just beyond. Enter the door marked Administrative Offices and ask about seeing the temple. In this sanctuary, Sikh scripture is read day and night over a four-day period each week. The murals and artworks here are extraordinary. A mural behind the altar depicts the well-known Sikh symbol of a serpent curling around a dagger, representing Kundalini energy. Sunday services are open to the public and are followed by a vegetarian meal.

After your stop at the temple, head back along the route you came in on. However, once you have driven through the hill again, instead of heading back to US 84/285, turn right for a second quick sight. About one third of a mile further, on your left, is a large building set back off the road. An arch over its driveway proclaims, "Hacienda de Guru Ram Dass." This is the residence of Yogi Bhajan. Here he spends about half the year; during the other half he's at his ashram in India. From the road, take note of the statuary, both in the yard and in the adjacent orchard.

Sikh Dharma International sponsors an annual week-long conference for Sikhs from all over the world during the time of the summer solstice. At this conference, held on land they own in the Jemez Mountains, one day is set aside as World Peace Prayer Day. Leaders of many different religious groups are asked to speak and the public is invited to attend at no charge. To contact the Sikh community, call (505) 753-5881.

Site 3: Cities of Gold Casino 🍂 *Try Your Luck!*

Get yourself back to US 84/285 and turn left. Approximately six miles down the road on the right you will see the exit for NM 502, the route you followed to San Ildefonso and Puye Cliffs. At this point you're back to the Cities of Gold Casino at Pojoaque Pueblo, now on your left.

Feeling lucky—or feeling hungry? Here is your chance to take part in the new "Buffalo Economy," where the thundering of coins has replaced the thundering of hooves. Indian gaming has become a source of controversy in numerous states around the country, and New Mexico is no exception. Complex issues relating to Native American sovereignty and the general economic impact of gambling on the fiscal health of states and local businesses have come to the fore. The debate rages on, but at this writing the slot machines are still gobbling up coins.

A distant cousin to Las Vegas gambling dens is Pojoaque's Cities of Gold Casino. At this writing, it features hundreds of slot machines, a craps table, roulette wheel, and special poker room. Chinese, Mexican, Italian, and Cajun favorites appear on a menu at very modest prices. Open 24 hours a day, you can get breakfast, lunch or dinner, and maybe your child's college tuition.

Leaving the casino, continue south on US 84/285 towards Santa Fe. Soon you depart Pojoaque Pueblo land and once again enter the home of the Tesuque people. Keep an eye out for **Camel Rock** on the right side of the thoroughfare. As you approach this natural sandstone sculpture, with the Tesuque R.V. Campground on your right, the camel "disappears" and something new takes shape. When the camel's hump is blocked by its head, some people see another creature. (Here's a hint: this endearing character appeared in one of Steven Spielberg's greatest money-making films, and is identified by two initials.)

Continue for three and one-half miles, passing Billco Carpets and the Tesuque Pueblo entrance. Now move into the left lane and look for a sign for the left-hand turn to the village of **Tesuque**. Be patient, and *careful*: it may take a few moments to cross the highway if northbound traffic is heavy. Once across the highway, you are on your way into this charming and peaceful village.

Follow this road for about one and one half miles to the tiny commercial district, which consists of El Nido restaurant and Tesuque Village Market. A green sign across from El Nido indicates a left fork turn onto Bishops Lodge Road. Take that fork. Within 200 feet you will come to an intersection. Tesuque Village Market, a good place for snacks or a quick sandwich or burrito, is just to your right off this short intersecting road.

You've visited a small Indian village (San Ildefonso) and a small Hispanic village (Abiquiu). Now you can visit another small village, originally Hispanic, now predominantly Anglo. The Tesuque hamlet has become a mecca for those who wish to live in a pastoral rural setting near Santa Fe. Hidden in the surrounding hills are many beautiful homes, including properties owned by such celebrities as Gene Hackman, Ali McGraw, Marsha Mason, Robert Redford, and

James Taylor. The population of Tesuque doubled to about 1500 in the past ten years. One of its draws (beside easy access to Santa Fe) is its country-like character, ideal for those who own and ride horses. The leafy trees and lush fields are in marked contrast to most of the landscape you've been seeing on this one-day trip. To many visitors, it suggests verdant farm country found in states east of the Mississippi River.

Leaving the village center, 1/10 mile on your left you will see a sign reading "Woodcarving." This is the studio of **Ben Ortega**, a well-known *santero* (artist who carves or paints religious images). Ortega is famous for rustic tree-trunk images of St. Francis, the patron saint of Santa Fe. He has won many awards at Spanish Market, a popular arts and craft festival held in Santa Fe each July.

Stop 4: Shidoni Foundry and Gallery

Right after Ben Ortega's is the Tesuque Elementary School. Continue traveling on Bishops Lodge Road for less than a mile until you see signs for Shidoni, located on your right.

Ancient peoples carved images on rocks that have survived the vagaries of time and weather. At Shidoni, contemporary sculptors also craft images they hope will endure—they're casting them in bronze!

Shidoni Foundry and Gallery is well worth a look. This facility includes a foundry, two galleries and two large sculpture gardens. Shidoni (a word used when Navajos meet and greet) spreads across eight acres near the Tesuque River on the site of a former apple orchard and chicken farm.

As you enter the dirt drive, a parking lot with a gallery featuring contemporary works is to the left. The first of two large sculpture gardens lies just beyond it, with monumental pieces in steel, bronze and mixed media—some representational, some abstract. By following the lane leading to the rear of the sculpture garden, you arrive at the foundry, and a smaller gallery featuring bronzes. To the right is the other sculpture garden. Ambling through these gardens beneath the blue New Mexico sky is exhilarating. You may want to return for a picnic with these bronze beauties; a few tables for just this purpose are provided.

The foundry, continuing to grow after more than a quarter century, employs more than 40 skilled craftspeople, many of whom are sculptors in their own right. These artisans practice the ancient technique of lost-wax bronze casting. Dramatic pourings of liquid bronze, heated to 1400 degrees, may be observed on Saturdays. Go early; space is limited. Call (505) 988-8001 for pouring times and other information.

We think you'll likely say goodbye to Shidoni with reluctance! Turn right onto Bishops Lodge Road and drive for approximately two miles until you see the sign for Bishops Lodge. The country lane you're on meanders on a narrow course, so watch for oncoming traffic which can include lumbering tour buses. On the way to the Bishops Lodge, glance up to the hills on your right. A striking adobe home set high in the hill will come into view. It's an example of the newer high-end homes ($500,000-plus) that have been built in Tesuque in the last decade.

Site 5: Bishops Lodge 🐾 *A Holy Resort*

For over a decade, the *Mobil Travel Guide* has listed Bishops Lodge as one of the Southwest's finest ranch resorts, awarding it a four-star rating. The lodge caters to families, offering good food, swimming, hiking, tennis, horseback riding, and a wonderfully relaxed atmosphere. Non-guests may also ride here but reservations are required. The Thorpe family has been operating this vacation Eden since 1918.

The white chapel spire, visible from the road, marks the heart of the former retreat of Archbishop Jean Baptiste Lamy, the first Catholic bishop in the Southwest. Father Lamy, an erudite Frenchman, was selected by American clergy to minister to a distant, poor and predominantly Hispanic community in 1850. Such a combination during Lamy's 35-year tenure has given historians and authors much to write about. Willa Cather's historical novel, *Death Comes for the Archbishop*, is an imaginative work about the archbishop's experience in New Mexico.

Calling his retreat *La Villa Pintoresca* (Italian for picturesque villa), Lamy purchased this property of some 600 acres for $80 in the 1860s. The prelate built a small chapel with an attached bedroom and sitting room. Archbishop Lamy was said to have walked the three miles from Santa Fe to this weekend retreat, where he gardened and planted fruit trees.

You may visit the chapel, now a National Historic Landmark, by requesting a key at the registration desk of the lodge. It is so charming you may be tempted to get married here or renew your wedding vows. Perhaps the honeymoon suite is available! Call the Bishops Lodge at (505) 983-6377.

Santa Fe awaits just over the next ridge. If you drove into the lodge, exit by turning left back onto Bishops Lodge Road and begin ascending the ridge. You will soon see the Santa Fe city limits sign on the right. The houses on the ridge, on your left-hand side, are on Brownell Howland Drive, a dirt road. Living on a dirt road in Santa Fe is said to be more prestigious than living on a paved road—homes here reach seven figures.

This ridge in the 1920s and 30s was the homesite of two Santa Fe socialites, Eleanor Brownell and Alice Howland. They were associated with an early gay movement that developed in Santa Fe about the same time the art colony arose. During this era, a women's watering hole was established in an adobe house on Canyon Road. Some recall that in the bar's early days when a white flag was displayed it signified that men were also welcome on the premises. Or perhaps that's just another of Santa Fe's colorful legends. Claude's Bar (named for its female proprietress) catered predominantly to the bohemian crowd into the 1960s.

Once over the ridge, a view of Santa Fe spreads out before you. As you descend into the city, Artist Road takes off on your left and becomes Hyde Park Road a little further on. If you drive 15 miles up this mountain road, you pass through Hyde State Park (a sylvan camping and recreation area), ponderosa forests and aspen groves, arriving finally at the **Santa Fe Ski Basin**.

In winter, skiers may purchase an adult full-day ticket for under $40; discounted rates are offered for seniors and children. Rental equipment runs from $15 per day. In summer, stunning views of the surrounding alpine wilderness can be enjoyed from the Basin's ski lifts. Rides continue from the Fourth of July weekend through Labor Day, as well as during the colorful aspen season (late September through mid-October) when the leaves turn a shimmering gold. Round-trip rides cost $6, with a one-way charge of $4 in case you'd like to step out for a lovely hike down the mountain. For schedule information call (505) 983-9155; the same number provides snow reports in winter.

From Artist Road it's just a quarter mile around the next curve to where you'll come upon the large pink **Scottish Rite Temple**, a Masonic hall modeled after the Alhambra in Granada, Spain—and an example of Moorish influence in Santa Fe. At the stoplight you'll have returned to Paseo de Peralta.

Your day's journey is complete! We hope it will live long and with pleasure in your memories. Remember, in Santa Fe the flag is always out—for men, women and kids alike. You are always welcome!

¡Un día perfecto en el norte de Nuevo México!
(A perfect day in northern New Mexico!)

APPENDICES

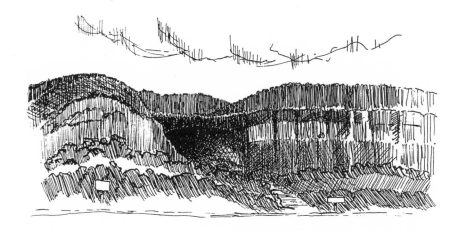

Glossary and Pronunciation Guide

Acequia (ah *SAY* key ah). Irrigation ditch created and maintained by Spanish farming communities to distribute water resources fairly.

Adobe (ah *DOE* bay). Construction material composed of earth (mostly clay and sand), water and straw, then dried in the sun.

Anasazi (ah nah *SAH* zee). People of a prehistoric culture who are believed to be the ancestors of the modern Pueblo people.

Anglo (*AN* glo). In New Mexico, generally a person who is neither Hispanic nor Native American.

Arroyo (ah *ROY* yo). Usually dry natural water course, at times awash from heavy rainfalls or runoff. Called a wash or gully elsewhere.

Brujos (*BREW* hose). Witches. Often included in legends and folk tales of both Hispanic and Indian cultures.

Cacique (ka *SEE* kay). In Pueblo communities, the spiritual leader and repository of religious traditions.

Chamisa (cha *ME* sah). A gray-green plant with golden flower heads that bloom in early fall. Found along roadsides and arroyos, chamisa is also known as rabbitbrush.

Cholla (*CHOY* yah). Shrub-like cactus which may have red, orange, purple, or yellow flowers when in bloom.

Cibola (*SEE* bow lah). A mythical province or city of gold, purported to have been established by seven Portuguese priests west of Spain and Portugal.

Coeloyphysis (see low *FIE* sis). A small dinosaur that lived 200 million years ago, fossils of which have been found at Ghost Ranch in New Mexico. State fossil of New Mexico.

Confraternity (con frah *TER* nee tee). A brotherhood created with a special interest which can have a professional or religious agenda.

Dar al-Islam (dar al is *LAM*). Arabic translation: Place of Surrender. Name of Islamic foundation in Abiquiu (see *Part Four*).

Genízaro (hay *NEE* sah roe). Native American kidnapped by nomadic Indians, such as the Comanches. Ransomed to Hispanic families where they were baptized, given the family name and employed as servants for a prescribed period of time. Genízaros were often later used by Spanish governors as buffer settlers on the frontier.

Hasira (ha *SEE* rah). Straw prayer rugs found in a mosque.

Horno (*OR* no). Beehive-shaped earthen oven used for baking purposes, introduced to the Southwest by the Spanish.

Kiva (*KEY* vah). Ceremonial chamber, often round and subterranean, used almost exclusively by male Pueblo tribal members.

Madressah (mah *DRESS* ah). Islamic word for study facility.

Mano, Metate (*MAH* no, may *TAH* tay). Stone tools for grinding corn.

Massid (mah *SEED*). Islamic word for mosque.

Morada (mo *RAH* dah). A sanctuary used by the Penitentes.

Otowi (*OH* toe wee). Tewa Indian word for "a place where the river makes a noise." Name of Anasazi ruin and nearby bridge.

Penitente (pen ee *TEN* tay). Member of lay Catholic brotherhood that practices corporeal penance, and in the past preserved Catholic traditions in the absence of priests.

Petroglyphs (*PET* roe gliffs). Pecked images on rocks left by Archaic and Anasazi peoples in New Mexico.

Poshuouinge (poh shoe o *WIN* gay). "Village above muddy water," a large ruin near Abiquiu.

Posole (poh *SO* lay). Corn soaked in lime (hominy) and prepared with meat in a stew.

P'o Suwae Geh (poh sue *WHY* gay). "A place to drink water." Tewa name for Pojoaque Pueblo (see *Part One*).

Pojoaque (poh *WAH* kay). Spanish spelling and pronunciation for Tewa pueblo north of Santa Fe.

Po Woh Ge Oweenge (poh woe gay oh *WEAN* gay). "Where the water cuts through." Tewa name for San Ildefonso Pueblo.

Pueblo (*PWAY* blo). "Town." Spanish name for New Mexico's Indian villages and the people who inhabit them.

Puye (*POO* jay, or *POO* yay). "A place where rabbits gather." Anasazi ruins on Santa Clara Pueblo land (see *Part Two*).

Sopaipilla (sow pah *PEE* yah). Puffy, lightly deep-fried bread, usually served with honey, accompanying the entree in New Mexican cuisine.

Tesuque (teh *SUE* kay). Spanish spelling and pronunciation for Tewa pueblo just north of Santa Fe.

Te Tsu Geh (tay *TSUE* gay). "Cottonwood tree place." Tewa name for Tesuque Pueblo (see *Part One*).

Tewa (*TAY* wah). Language of six pueblos north of Santa Fe. Part of Tanoan language group that also includes Tiwa and Towa tongues.

Tuff. Soft volcanic ash that has been solidified. Rock material of the cave dwellings of the Rio Grande Anasazi.

Viga (*VEE* gah). Roof beams made from stripped pine tree trunks in Pueblo, Spanish and today's Santa Fe style homes.

Calendar of Pueblo Events

ALTHOUGH dates of feast days do not change from year to year, dates and times of other dances may be subject to change with very little notice. Contact the Governor's Office of the pueblo you are planning to visit to make sure dances will be held on the scheduled day. The events below are at the pueblos along or close to our route. Here are the numbers for all eight Northern Pueblos: Picuris, (505) 852-4275; Pojoaque, 455-2278; Nambe, 455-2036; San Ildefonso, 455-2273; San Juan, 852-4265; Santa Clara, 753-7330; Taos, 758-9593; Tesuque, 983-2667.

DATE	EVENT	PUEBLO
Jan 1 or Jan 6	Transfer of Canes, various dances, King's Day (in honor of new tribal officers)	Most Pueblos
Jan 22	Bonfire Deer Dance	San Ildefonso
Jan 23	San Ildefonso Feast Day	San Ildefonso
Feb 2	Various dance	Most Pueblos
2nd wk Feb	Deer Dance	San Juan
Easter	Various dances	Most Pueblos
Memorial Day Weekend	Inter-Tribal Powwow	Pojoaque
June 13	St. Anthony's Feast Day	Santa Clara
June 23-24	San Juan Feast Day	San Juan
July 4	Nambe Falls Celebration	Nambe
July 15-16	Pueblo Artist and Craftsman Show	Santa Clara
Early Aug	Appreciation Day	Pojoaque
Aug 12	Santa Clara Pueblo Feast Day	Santa Clara
August	Indian Market	Santa Fe
Aug-Sept	Corn Dances	San Ildefonso
Oct 3-4	St. Francis of Assisi Feast Day	Nambe
Nov 12	San Diego Feast Day	Tesuque
Dec 12	Guadalupe Feast Day	Pojoaque
Dec 24	Sundown Torchlight Procession	San Juan
Dec 25	Vespers and Matachinas Dance	Various Pueblos
Dec 26	Turtle Dance	San Juan
Dec 28	Holy Innocents Day	Santa Clara

Pueblo Etiquette

HERE'S what you should know, according to the *1995 Visitor's Guide*, published by the Eight Northern Indian Pueblos:

1. Each pueblo operates under its own government and establishes its own rules for visitors. Please obey all rules and regulations of the individual pueblos.

2. Please control your children and see that they are respectful.

3. Although most pueblos are open to the public during daylight hours, the homes are private. Do not enter any without an invitation.

4. Please stay in the immediate village area. Do not climb walls or other structures. Some are several hundred years old and damage easily.

5. Do not pick up or remove any artifacts or objects, such as pieces of broken pottery.

6. Kivas and graveyards are *not* to be entered by non-Pueblo people.

7. Alcohol, weapons and drugs will not be tolerated.

8. No pets, please.

9. Please obey all traffic, parking and speed limit signs. Our children are at play, and many of our people are elderly.

Hiking Possibilities

HIKING in the forests and canyons of northern New Mexico is surely one of the most attractive activities nature provides here. For those who wish to hike, we recommend the local Sierra Club publication *Day Hikes in the Santa Fe Area*. It contains information on over 35 hikes, including degree of difficulty, estimated time, length of trail, elevations hiked through, and detailed directions to the trailhead.

Along the route there are several hikes that can be included—either in this day's itinerary, or on a separate outing. At Plaza Blanca (*Part Four*), you can wander among the unusual, natural mud formations. A narrow path at the parking area will lead you into Plaza Blanca. Thereafter there are no trails, but the terrain is basically flat, making exploration easy.

At Ghost Ranch (*Part Five*) three hikes offer fabulous views as well as a cardiovascular workout. The Ghost Ranch Conference Center requests that all hikers on their property register at the office. There you can get details about these three quite different hikes, and use the restrooms.

The Kitchen Mesa hike at Ghost Ranch is one of our favorites. After passing the "dinosaur quarry," the trail quickly gets you into what feels like a remote canyon, though it is not far from civilization at Ghost Ranch. Although the hiking is generally easy, in order to get on Kitchen Mesa you have to climb a steep incline and make your way up a rock crevice. If you make it, you will be rewarded by a heart-stopping vista from the white gypsum capstone on top. Even if you don't make it up the crevice, the hike in the canyon is a time you will remember.

Off the main route, but not too far away, are other opportunities to stretch your legs. These trails might better be left for another day, however, if you plan to cover the suggested route. The Santa Fe National Forest has created numerous trails through the aspen and evergreen forests along the road to, and at the Santa Fe Ski Basin.

On the way to Bandelier National Monument are two excellent hikes to Anasazi ruins: Otowi Ruins Trail at the junction of N.M.502 and N.M.4, and Tsankawi Ruins, one mile beyond on N.M.4. Bandelier itself has about 70 miles of hiking and backcountry camping.

Finally, you can climb Cerro Pedernal ("Georgia O'Keeffe's mountain," see *Part Four*) by turning off U.S.84 onto N.M.96 at Abiquiu Reservoir. In order to explore these areas, you will need your hiking book and or topo maps and information from Santa Fe National Forest, (505) 988-6940, or the National Park Service, (505) 988-6100.

Be sure to heed warnings about the weather, especially in spring and fall when a pleasant afternoon can turn quickly into a blinding snowstorm. Carry water and a jacket or sweater at all times.

Happy hiking!

Birding in New Mexico's High Desert

YOU'RE IN what people here call the High Desert—not exactly the parched and barren land the word "desert" commonly brings to mind. Santa Fe receives an average yearly rainfall of 14 to 15 inches; Española, 25 miles away, gets a little less. And the mountain tops (above 10,000 feet) get 30 to 40 inches annually. Piñon pine, juniper, ponderosa, aspen and fir make their home here—not creosote or ocotillo and prickly pear cactus common in the low desert of southern New Mexico.

But for the most part northern New Mexico is generally arid, with few large bodies of water, thus limiting the kind and count of feathered residents. Although New Mexico has fewer birds per acre than many states, those we do have are easier to see because of sparse and rather scrawny vegetation. Also, New Mexico is on a major north-south flyway, so many birds stop by in spring and fall.

To accompany a birding guide of North America, curious birders should get a copy of the *New Mexico Bird Finding Guide*, published by the New Mexico Ornithological Society. Therein you'll find detailed directions and likely sightings at locations throughout the state. Here we suggest just a few birding opportunities to whet the appetite of bird lovers, both serious and not so serious.

Throughout *From Santa Fe to O'Keeffe Country* we have mentioned spots along the route to look for birds. Riparian areas are generally the best locations to find a variety of birds.

Two good options along the route: First, from the Cities of Gold Casino in Pojoaque (*Part One*) take N.M.502 one half mile beyond its intersection with U.S.84/285. At the first right, turn and proceed one-tenth mile. There make a left turn and follow the dirt road along the almost dry Tesuque River. In summer look for *greater roadrunner* (the state bird), *scaled* and *Gambel's quail, northern rough-winged* and *barn swallows, loggerhead shrike, black-headed* and *blue grosbeaks* and *canyon towhee*, among over 25 species that can be seen.

Second, the drive to Abiquiu that parallels the Chama River (*Parts Two, Three and Four*) is an excellent stretch on which to find *bald eagles* perched in cottonwoods in winter. Two miles beyond the junction of N.M.110 and U.S.84, the Chama River makes a large bend near the roadside. *Common mergansers* and *common goldeneyes* are often among the wintering waterfowl at this site. Look for *great blue herons* at waters edge and *bald eagles* in the nearby trees. The actual setting for Georgia O'Keeffe's Blue River paintings (about four miles northwest of Abiquiu, (Site 4 in *Part Four*) is a good spot to scan the trees and cliffs for eagles. Abiquiu Reservoir provides overlooks where spotting scopes can be used to seek wintering birds on the open water. Proceeding toward Ghost Ranch, the fences and electrical poles may be resting spots for *red-tailed* and *ferruginous hawks, golden eagles* or rare wintering *rough-legged hawks* and *merlins*.

If you are based in Santa Fe, you have the wonderful resource of the **Randall Davey Audubon Center**, a National Audubon Society facility, at the end of Canyon Road in the eastern foothills. There you can wander on 135 acres of woodland at the mouth of Santa Fe Canyon, buy books, get tips of recent bird sightings of note, and maybe join an Audubon field trip, (505) 983-4609.

Three other quick suggestions off the general route: **Bandelier National Monument**, about 20 miles beyond the N.M.30 turnoff after Otowi bridge (*Part Two*), is the major birding site of the area. The **Santa Fe Ski Basin** (16 miles from the Plaza) provides great montane birds in summer, including *red-naped* and *Williamson's sapsuckers, red crossbills* and *dusky flycatchers*. Finally, a bit further afield, the **Bosque del Apache** is the spectacular winter home for zillions of ducks, *snow geese, sandhill cranes* (a few *whoopers*, too!) and raptors from November to February. Charles Kuralt, in his best seller, *Charles Kuralt's America*, selected the Bosque del Apache as his featured location for November, one of his twelve favorite places in America.

Restaurant Recommendations

WE HAVE SAMPLED most of these restaurants and have strong recommendations for the others. Most do not require reservations and you'll find that prices are generally more appetizing than at Santa Fe's eateries. If you find the chile daunting (its virtually an addiction with New Mexicans of all walks of life), cold milk or traditional sopaipillas smothered with honey will tame the flames. Care to mix your red and green chile? Ask for "Christmas."

ABIQUIU AREA:

Abiquiu Inn

US 84, about ½ mile south of Abiquiu, (505) 685-4378. Summer hours for breakfast, 7:30 to 10:30 a.m.; lunch, 11:30 a.m. to 4 p.m.; dinner, 5 to 9 p.m. Off-season hours are shorter, so call ahead.

Breakfast, lunch and dinner, with snacks in between.

Bode's Deli

US 84, Bode's General Store, Abiquiu, (505) 685-4422.

Homemade sandwiches, salads and baked goods. Perfect for picnics.

La Cocinita

US 84, 2 miles south of Abiquiu, (505) 685-4609. Lunch and early dinner.

Good New Mexican food at reasonable prices.

Trade Routes Bazaar and Coffee House

US 84, midway between mile markers 210 and 211, approximately one mile south of Abiquiu (look for the coffee cup on the roof), (505) 685-4790. Open 8 a.m. to 7 p.m. (summer); 9 a.m. to 5 p.m. (winter).

Light lunches, bagels, specialty coffees, teas, sodas, and deserts. In summer, a fresh juice and tonic bar is open outside as well. Local singers, poets and writers perform.

ESPANOLA AND ENVIRONS:

Anthony's at the Delta

228 Oñate NW (US 84/285 west of Rio Grande (see *Part Two* map), (505) 753-4511. Dinner only; reservations suggested.

Fine dining in an elegant New Mexican setting. Offers both American and local fare. Prices are not exorbitant but probably the most expensive of our recommendations.

El Paragua

Just off NM 68 on NM 76 in Española, (505) 753-8852. Lunch and dinner 11 a.m. to 8:30 p.m. Sunday through Thursday; 11 a.m. to 9 p.m. Friday through Saturday.

Wonderful northern New Mexico food, satisfying palettes for over 30 years. Light lunches as well as full dinners are offered. The sopaipillas and chiles rellenos are highly recommended.

Gabriel's

On US 84/285, 3 miles south of Pojoaque Pueblo, (505) 455-7000. Lunch and dinner 11:30 a.m. to 9 p.m. Thursday through Sunday; 11:30 a.m. to 10 p.m. Friday and Saturday.

As you sip your ice-cold Margaritas, your order of guacamole (made with three avocados and your choice of fresh ingredients) is being prepared in a metate at your table. Crisply-baked tortilla chips accompany the dish. One order will serve four people ($7.50). New Mexican and Mexican items complete the menu.

Jo Ann's Rancho-O-Casados

411 North Riverside, Española, (505) 753-2837. Breakfast, lunch and dinner 8 a.m. to 8:30 p.m. (closed Sundays).

Nothing bought that can't be grown fresh on the family-owned farm. Jo Ann serves dishes that have attracted the likes of Spanish royalty, and such celebrities as Robert Redford and Lynda Carter. The carne adovada and award-winning chile make this eatery not to be missed. Jo Ann usually comes to your table to make sure you are satisfied.

Matilda's

Just off Riverside Drive (US 84/285) on Corlett Road, near the turnoff to Abiquiu and Ojo Caliente, (505) 753-3200. Open 9 a.m. to 9 p.m., closed Mondays.

Fabulous traditional New Mexican fare is made by Matilda. Unique green chile (see Part Six).

Rio Grande Cafe

Los Alamos Road, just south of the new community plaza. It's on the route between the two traffic lights in Española (see *Part Two* map on page 40), (505) 753-2125. Open 9 a.m. to 5 p.m. Monday through Friday.

If you can put aside your low cholesterol and non-meat diets, here is a place to find 12 different ways to have your enchiladas and choose from eight different Mexican beers. Open since the early 1950s, the cafe has become an institution for New Mexican food for locals and travelers. Its menu features dozens of New Mexican and American choices. The green chile is filled with beef and sandwiches come on white bread—hearkening back to cuisine of a more innocent era. The reasonable prices may remind you of the 50s as well.

Cuentos: Stories from Northern New Mexico

THE FOLLOWING stories are from *Cuentos: Tales from the Hispanic Southwest*, selected by Jose Griego y Maestas and retold in English by Rudolfo A. Anaya, published by the Museum of New Mexico Press. We've included them here because young children may be amused by them as you drive along:

LOS CUATRO ELEMENTOS
The Four Elements

In the beginning there were four elements on this earth, as well as in man. These basic elements were Water, Fire, Wind and Honor. When the work of the creation was completed, the elements decided to separate, with each one seeking its own way.

Water spoke first and said: "Our work in the creation of earth and man is done. Now it is proper to go our own ways, but if you should ever need me, look for me under the earth and in the oceans."

Fire then said, "We will separate forever, but if you should need me you will find me in steel and in the power of the sun."

Wind whispered, "If you should need me, I will be in the heavens among the clouds."

Honor was the last to speak, and it said, "I am the bond of life. If once you lose me don't look for me again—you will not find me!"

EL PERICO QUE COMPRÓ LEÑA
The Parrot Who Bought Firewood

When the first snow powdered the Sangre de Cristo Mountains and the cold winds whistled through the valley and froze the Santa Fe River, the men who sold firewood would load their burros with wood and go through the streets of Santa Fe selling wood.

One day two wood vendors passed by the plaza and stopped near the house of a man who bought from them regularly. Now it so happened that no one was home, but the woman of the house had a parrot who spoke many words in Spanish.

The parrot had seen and heard his master buy firewood many times before, so when the vendors called, "*¡Leña, leña para vender!*" the parrot whistled and answered, "*¡Si, compro leña!*"—Yes, I'll buy some firewood!

The vendors thought it was the master of the house who had shouted out that he wanted firewood, so they unloaded their burros at the wood-pile. But when they went to collect for the wood no one answered the door, so they decided to return that afternoon for their pay.

"But I didn't buy firewood," the master of the house said. "Someone shouted from the house that you needed wood," the vendors insisted.

Then the woman remembered that she had left the parrot out of his cage, and she suspected that he had been the one who had bought the wood. So they paid for the firewood, and the woman scolded the parrot who then sulked off down to the cellar.

Meanwhile, the cat climbed up on the table and took a piece of the meat the man had bought in town. When the woman saw what the cat had done she turned to punish him and threw him into the cellar.

When the parrot saw the cat tossed into the cellar for his misdeed, he chuckled and said, "What happened? Did you buy firewood too?"

Recommended Reading

Archaeology

Ferguson, William, and Arthur H. Rohn. *Anasazi Ruins of the Southwest*. University of New Mexico Press, Albuquerque, 1987.

Stuart, David E. *The Magic of Bandelier*. Ancient City Press, Santa Fe, 1989.

Art and Architecture

Blair, M.E., and Lawrence R. Blair. *Margaret Tofoya, A Tewa Potter's Heritage and Legacy*. Shiffler Publishing, West Chester, Pennsylvania, 1986.

Bry, Doris, and Nicholas Callaway. *Georgia O'Keeffe: In the West*. Alfred A. Knopf, New York, 1989.

Cowart, Jack, Juan Hamilton and S. Greenough. *Georgia O'Keeffe: Art and Letters*. National Gallery of Art, Washington, 1987.

Dillingham, Rick. *Fourteen Families in Pueblo Pottery*. University of New Mexico Press, Albuquerque, 1994.

Eldredge, Charles C. *Georgia O'Keeffe, American and Modern*. Yale University Press, New Haven, 1993.

Eldredge, Charles C. *Georgia O'Keeffe*. Harry N. Abrams, Inc., New York, 1991.

Romero, Orlando, and David Larkin. *Adobe: Building a Living with the Earth*. Houghton Mifflin Co., Boston, 1994.

Biography

Dawson, Robert. *Ansel Adams, New Light: Essays on His Legacy and Legend*. Friends of Photography, San Francisco, 1993.

Hogrefe, Jeffrey. *O'Keeffe, The Life of an American Legend*. Bantam Books, New York, 1994.

Lisle, Laurie. *Portrait of an Artist, A Biography of Georgia O'Keeffe*. Washington Square Press, New York, 1986.

Lynes, Barbara Buhler. *O'Keeffe, Steiglitz and the Critics, 1916-1929*. University of Chicago Press, Chicago 1989.

Peterson, Susan. *The Living Tradition of Maria Martinez*. Kodanski International, Tokyo and New York, 1977.

Birds, Botany and Ethnobiology

Dunmire, William W. and Gail D. Tierney. *Wild Plants of the Pueblo Province.* Museum of New Mexico Press, Santa Fe, 1995.

Zimmerman, Dale A., *et al. New Mexico Bird Finding Guide.* New Mexico Ornithological Society, Albuquerque, 1992.

Culture

Chavez, Angelico. *My Penitente Land.* University of New Mexico Press, Albuquerque, 1974.

Griego y Maestas, Jose and Rudolfo A. Anaya. *Cuentos: Tales from the Hispanic Southwest.* Museum of New Mexico Press, Santa Fe, 1980.

Gutierrez, Ramon A. *When Jesus Came, the Corn Mothers Went Away— Marriage, Sexuality and Power in New Mexico: 1500-1846.* University of California Press, Berkeley, 1991.

Roediger, Virginia More. *Ceremonial Costumes of the Pueblo Indians— Their Evolution, Fabrication, and Significance in the Prayer Drama.* University of California Press, Berkeley, 1941.

Weatherford, Jack. *Indian Givers: How the Indians of the Americas Transformed the World.* Fawcett Columbine, New York, 1988.

Geology and Paleontology

Chronic, Halka. *Roadside Geology of New Mexico.* Mountain Press Publishing, Missoula, 1987.

Lucas, Spencer G. *Dinosaurs of New Mexico.* New Mexico Academy of Science, Albuquerque, 1993.

Ratkevich, Ronald Paul. *Dinosaurs of the Southwest.* University of New Mexico Press, Albuquerque, 1976.

Hiking

Evans, Harry. *Fifty Hikes in New Mexico.* Gem Guides Books, Co., Baldwin Park, Calif., 1995.

The Sierra Club. *Day Hikes in the Santa Fe Area.* The Santa Fe Group of the Sierra Club, Santa Fe, 1995.

History

Church, Peggy Pond. *The House at Otowi Bridge*. University of New Mexico Press, Albuquerque, 1960.

Horgan, Paul. *Great River: The Rio Grande in North American History*. University Press of New England, Hanover, N.H., 1984.

Sando, Joe. *Pueblo Nations: Eight Centuries of Pueblo Indian History*. Clear Light Publishers, Santa Fe, 1992.

Simmons, Marc. *New Mexico: An Interpretive History*. University of New Mexico Press, Albuquerque, 1991.

Novels

Cather, Willa. *Death Comes for the Archbishop*. Vintage Books, New York, 1990.

Laughlin, Ruth. *The Wind Leaves No Shadow*. Caxton Printers, Ltd., Caldwell, Idaho, 1986.

Waters, Frank. *People of the Valley*. Sage Books, Denver, 1941.

Waters, Frank. *Woman at Otowi Crossing*. Ohio University Press, Athens, Ohio, 1987.

NOTES ❧